Front cover

Group of dolls 1780–1902: (far left) a wax portrait figure of Edward VII of 1901–2, attributed to the Pierotti family; (top left) a poured-wax doll of 1884–87 by John Edwards; (top right) large doll of 1823–32, see doll 12; (far right) a poured-wax doll of 1868–72, attributed to the Marsh family; (centre right) boy doll of 1865–70, see doll 27; (centre) royal bride doll of 1863, see doll 33; (centre left) wooden doll of 1780–90, see doll 8; (lower left) novelty group of dolls of 1860–65, see dolls 30; (bottom, left and right) dolls dressed by Princess Victoria and her governess in 1831–33, see dolls 10.

Inside front cover (left)

Group of small wooden dolls dressed in 1830–33 by Princess Victoria and her governess to represent stars of ballets and operas performed in London.

Back cover

Poured-wax doll of 1882–84, wearing Court presentation dress of crimson velvet and fawn silk. This doll is believed to have been dressed by Madame Elise, a famous Court dressmaker, and may have been used to demonstrate a new fashion to her clients. (42cm)

THE MUSEUM OF LONDON 1986

The Museum of London is funded jointly by the Office of Arts & Libraries and the Corporation of the City of London

© Copyright Museum of London 1986

Text by Caroline Goldthorpe & Kay Staniland
Photography by John Edwards & Susan Seright
Designed by David Challis
Production by Jenny Hall & Jane Morris
Printed in England by Jolly & Barber Limited, Rugby

ISBN 0 904818 26 8

1 Child doll of 1700–10, of painted wood with remnants of brown wig. Her blue, yellow and red striped silk robe is embroidered with red tulips and has leading strings; she wears white suede mittens and knitted pink silk stockings. (38cm)

(Measurements refer to height of dolls)

DOLLS

A SELECTION 1700 TO 1910

Cherished companions of childhood, dolls have a history extending back into antiquity. Rag dolls were replaced by stylized wooden dolls, and sixteenth-century portraits show small girls clutching elaborately-dressed miniature likenesses. The earliest surviving examples in Britain are of late seventeenth-century date. At some point skilled wax modellers began making dolls, but these were very fragile playthings until methods of reinforcing the wax were introduced in the nineteenth century.

Little is known of the makers of early dolls in London up to the mid nineteenth century, but they were an important small industry supplying the majority of goods in the metropolis. The wax doll-makers predominated, and increasingly wooden dolls were imported from Germany, together with moulded papier-mâché dolls made from pulped paper mixed with various binding agents. These, like the wax dolls, usually had heads and limbs attached to a stuffed cloth body, allowing a factory system to develop. Greater realism was attempted and some early nineteenth-century doll-makers experimented with eye-movements by extending a wire down through the doll's body.

The greatest impetus for London's expanding doll industry, where ingenuity, novelty and popular appeal were vital, came from Queen Victoria and her young family. They inspired such famous exponents of the art of wax-modelling as the Pierotti and Montanari families, John Edwards, Charles Marsh, and others. This was the peak period of the English doll-making industry. As the nineteenth century progressed it was increasingly threatened, and eventually completely undermined, by the beautiful porcelain dolls imported from France and Germany where mass-production factory techniques enabled their sophisticated products to compete successfully in world markets.

2

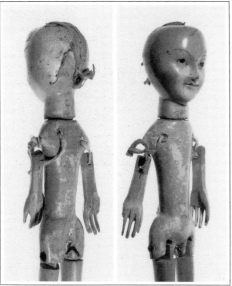

5 Detail of large wooden doll of 1745–55, showing her carefully-made underwear, miniature replicas of adult clothing: a lace-trimmed chemise of fine linen, and stays of silk stiffened with whalebone held between lines of stitching, possibly professional work. Her dress, of dark green silk, could have been made from an old dress; her quilted petticoats were certainly made from worn remnants. A later addition to this doll's outfit is a frilled white cotton cap, to conceal her baldness. (52cm; lower legs missing)

3

2 Doll of 1690–1710, of turned and painted wood, with arms attached by rag ties slotted through holes in the shoulders; the jointed legs are a later replacement. A metal rod inserted through the body gave slight movement to the head, an early novelty reintroduced a century later. The surviving clothes comprise linen chemise, two petticoats, apron and cap and a yellow silk dress. (18cm to hips)

3 Child doll of 1750–60, with poured-wax head and arms, and glass eyes. She wears a satin cap (ornament later) and Spitalfields silk dress with leading strings. (23cm)

4 Fashion doll of 1755–65; solid wax head and limbs on wire frame, moulded and painted hair and glass eyes. She wears a formal Court dress of striped and brocaded silk. (18cm)

4

The creators of the earliest dolls are anonymous craftsmen who gave extra life to the rigid dolls by carving and painting features, later adding glass eyes, elaborate wigs and peg-joints; attractive and elaborate clothing made by skilled needle-women completed the effect. Wax, an ancient modelling material, was gradually adopted for more lifelike but more fragile dolls.

6 Large doll of 1755–60; of painted wood with glass eyes, wearing a sack dress with matching petticoat of pink and yellow figured Spitalfields silk and pink silk stays. Her underwear consists of fine linen chemise, utilitarian linen stays, three figured linen petticoats and a stiffened hoop of boldly striped linen. The earring, locket and wig are later additions and her face has been partly repainted. Her jointed wooden arms are unusual at this early stage. Known as 'The Queen of Denmark' since the 1820s the origins of this doll are a little difficult to disentangle. She is believed to have been given by an English princess to Elizabeth (b.1748), middle daughter of Thomas Sampson, at one time chaplain of the Royal Hospital at Chelsea; in 1759 the future George III acted as godfather to his youngest son. It is possible that this princess was George III's sister Caroline Matilda (1751–75) who married Christian VII, King of Denmark, in 1766. (55cm)

6

4

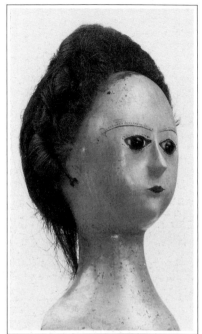

7 Head of wooden doll of 1765–70; original wig of grey-brown human hair, rolled above the forehead to resemble a fashionable adult wig. Most early dolls have lost their original hair through use. (52cm)

8 Painted wooden doll of 1780–90, with glass eyes and later wig and turban. Her white linen dress is trimmed with mauve and white silk ribbons and supported by a cane hoop. She wears fine white cotton stockings with blue silk garters matching her ribbon-trimmed white silk shoes. (28cm)

9 Child doll of 1815–20; painted wood with blue glass eyes with black pupils and later blonde wig. She has a dress of fine white organza with matching lace-trimmed pantalettes and a white wool petticoat; a bonnet, cape and boots of white satin complete her outfit. (27cm)

8

9

10 Between 1831 and 1833 Princess Victoria, soon to ascend the throne as Queen, worked with Baroness Lehzen her governess, and others, upon dressing a small army of wooden dolls which have become extremely famous through display in the London Museum. The dolls they used were of the stiff-jointed wooden type which sold widely for a few pence each; that they were so popular with a royal princess would have amazed their humble creators in the Alps. By far the largest group of dolls represent ladies of the nobility (far right and above). They are given titles which are mostly fictitious and it seems very likely that their dresses are based on those of ladies whom Princess Victoria admired. Sometimes the ladies were provided with several offspring, very tiny wooden dolls dressed to represent children, and babies made from stuffed cloth. Part of this group represents the Arnold family (near right foreground), but nothing is known now about who they may be; this family includes one of the very rare male dolls in the whole collection, Sir William Arnold, dressed by Baroness Lehzen. The second somewhat smaller group of dolls represents famous ballet dancers and opera singers. The Princess was allowed by her mother, the Duchess of Kent, frequently to visit the theatre and in these glamorous new productions, just being introduced to London audiences, this solitary young girl obviously found a delightful and engrossing world which she recorded energetically in her sketchbooks, diary and via these dolls. (heights of these dolls vary, but majority are about 17 cm) (see also Inside front cover)

6

11 *Austrian painted wooden doll dressed as a Welsh woman in striped wool bed-jacket, apron and petticoat. This doll was possibly given to Queen Victoria as a child when she visited Wales in August 1832 with her mother the Duchess of Kent. (38.5 cm)*

12 *Detail of large doll of 1828–32, with moulded papier-mâché head imitating elaborate fashionable coiffures; probably German. The doll is dressed as a child, with pantalettes of white cotton net matching her dress which has an underdress of deep pink cotton. (56 cm)*

13 *Papier-mâché headed doll of 1831–34, with stuffed cloth body. Her elegant light brown silk dress, pelerine and cream bonnet suggest that she was a fashion doll made by a milliner or a dressmaker; she carries an ornate net cap. The mass-production of papier-mâché heads, in the Sonneberg region of Germany, led to a rapid decline in the production of wooden dolls; both were superseded by wax and porcelain dolls. (28 cm)*

11

12

13

14 *Wax-over-papier-mâché doll of 1830–32, with blue glass eyes, elegant wig, and stuffed cloth body; her dress is of green silk. Dolls of this type were made in Clerkenwell and Shoreditch. (54cm)*

15 *Child doll of 1840–45; poured-wax with glass eyes and brown hair, possibly by the Pierotti family. The quality of her clothes suggest she was dressed professionally to be sold in one of London's famous toyshops. (53cm)*

16 *Charity-school doll with poured-wax head and arms, blue glass eyes and brown hair. She wears the uniform of the Female Orphan Asylum founded in Lambeth in 1758 by Sir John Fielding, brother of the novelist, and was probably dressed by one of the inmates in 1845. (52cm)*

17/18 Small German dolls of 1843–44 with solid wax heads and limbs, dressed to represent Queen Victoria's eldest children, and sold as souvenirs. The Prince of Wales wears a white organza dress and the Princess Royal's dress is of machine-lace over pale blue satin. (16.5cm, 15.5cm)

19 Seated baby doll with poured-wax head and limbs, blue glass eyes and fair hair. The doll, by Mme Augusta Montanari, was perhaps exhibited in the 1851 Great Exhibition and represented Queen Victoria's daughter the Princess Royal (as a baby) in 1841. The doll is exquisitely dressed in white cotton with lace insertions over pink satin, and pink ribbon trimmings. (seated height 36cm)

21 Large portrait doll of Queen Victoria, by Mme Montanari; possibly made for her prize-winning exhibit at the Great Exhibition in 1851. The figure has a poured-wax head and limbs, blue glass eyes, and ornately braided light brown human hair. Her dress is of fine pale blue silk ornamented with silk lace, her necklace is of gold braid and imitation pearls. Such dolls are distinctive for their exquisite clothing, and were extremely expensive. (61 cm)

22 Signature on body of above doll: 'Montanari, Soho Bazaar'. Opened in 1816, the Soho Bazaar in Soho Square sold fancy goods, including dolls by Mme Montanari and Charles Marsh.

23 Small German doll with solid wax head and limbs, given to eight year old Letitia Hawkins on 12 December 1852, the eve of her death. It is dressed in white and pink organza trimmed with green ribbon, and is still in its original paper-covered chip box. (14.5 cm)

24 Head of large portrait doll of Queen Victoria dressed in State robes of crimson velvet and ermine. It was probably exhibited by Mme Montanari in the Great Exhibition in 1851, where she was commended for 'the most remarkable and beautiful collection of Toys in the Great Exhibition'. (67 cm)

20 Boy doll with poured-wax head and arms on a stuffed cloth body, believed to be Queen Victoria's eldest son, the Prince of Wales (b.1841). It is possibly the work of the Pierotti family who had made and sold dolls in London since the 1790s. Dolls modelled on the Queen's children became very popular and this example, probably professionally dressed, represents the expensive end of the market. (47 cm)

25 Baby doll of 1850–60, with poured-wax
head and limbs, and dress of embroidered cotton
with a pink satin sash. 'FROM M NEEDHAM'
SOHO BAZAAR "WARRANTED TO STAND ANY
CLIMATE" Chas. MARSH MANUFACTURER
LONDON' stamped on the stuffed cloth body.
(51 cm)

27 Boy doll of 1865–70, with poured-wax
head and limbs, blue eyes and long brown
hair; possibly made by the London firm
of Pierotti. He wears a velvet knicker-
bocker suit trimmed with braid and glass
buttons. (42 cm)

26 Doll of 1860–70,
with poured-wax head
and limbs, blue eyes
and light brown hair,
wearing a dress of cream
cotton ornamented
with black velvet
ribbon and
glass buttons.
(56 cm)

25

26

27

28

29 Detail of doll with glazed porcelain head with painted features and moulded hair, on a fixed kid body. Dolls of this kind were a development of papier-mâché and were particularly popular from the 1840s to the 1860s. This example of 1855–60 wears a dress of white organza woven with pink spots and trimmed with silk ribbon. (37 cm)

30 Novelty group of dolls of 1860–65 set in a red leather shoe, depicting the nursery rhyme 'There was an old woman who lived in a shoe'. The larger dolls are of glazed porcelain, whilst the youngest children are jointed wooden dolls. (21 cm)

31 Box lid for mechanical walking doll of the type invented by Enoch Rice Morrison of New York and patented in 1862. The doll has a glazed porcelain head, stuffed leather arms and the metal feet are controlled by a clockwork mechanism concealed within a cardboard cone under the skirt. The fine blue silk dress of this example has disintegrated badly. (36.5 cm)

THE PATENT
AUTOPERIPATETIKOS
OR
WALKING·DOLL

MARTIN & RUNYON.

Office, 299 Broadway, New York.

DIRECTIONS
TO BE OBSERVED IN USING THE PATENT AUTOPERIPATETIKOS.

☞ In winding up, clasp the board at the bottom with the thumb and finger of the left hand.

1st.—With the right wind up, turning the key from you, and then set it LIGHTLY ON ITS FEET.

2d.—In all cases handle it only by the waist or bottom board.

3d.—If it should stop at any time, turn the feet toward you, and see if the inside leg is not caught against the boot.

4th.—Do not wind it too lightly.

28 Charity-school doll of 1860–70, with poured-wax head and composition limbs, blue glass eyes and fair hair. Her uniform consists of a green woollen dress, white cotton cap, tippet and apron, knitted mittens and brown leather shoes. She wears on a ribbon a medal inscribed with the Lord's Prayer, presented annually for good conduct. This is the indoor uniform of St Giles in the Fields and St George's Bloomsbury, instituted in 1705 and closed in 1921. (41 cm)

31

32 Doll with poured-wax head and limbs, dressed as Princess Louise on her marriage in 1871. It was probably dressed for salon use by a dressmaker. The dress is of white satin overlaid with flounces of Honiton lace. A body-stamp reads 'Peacocks, The Rocking Horse, 522 New Oxford Street, Corner of Bloomsbury, London W'. (46 cm)

33 Bisque-headed doll dressed as Princess Alexandra of Denmark, bride of the Prince of Wales in 1863. The white silk dress with cotton mesh and lace is an inaccurate representation but photographs were not widely available and many royal bride dolls are similarly inexact. (25 cm)

33

32

34 *Fashionable doll of 1865–70, with movable bisque head, blonde wig, and blue glass eyes set on fixed cream kid body; possibly by the French firm of Bru. She wears a lace-trimmed lime-green silk dress with a matching stylish hat, and blue leather boots. Possibly dressed professionally. (47 cm)*

35

35 *Rare bisque-headed 'Surprise Doll' patented by the Parisian firm of Bru in 1872. The doll has a light brown wig and dress of mauve satin trimmed with cream braid. The fully-articulated wooden body contains a clockwork musical box which plays several tunes. (44 cm)*

36 *The 'Surprise Doll' has its own wooden box with an illustration of a doll shop in the lid, and the label of 'William Whiteley, Universal Provider, Westbourne Grove, London, W'.*

36

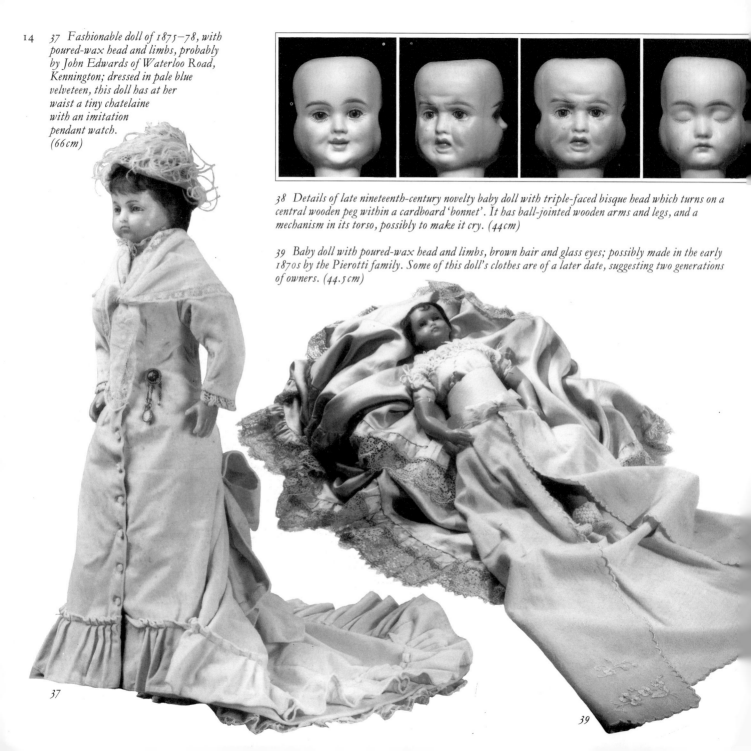

37 Fashionable doll of 1875–78, with poured-wax head and limbs, probably by John Edwards of Waterloo Road, Kennington; dressed in pale blue velveteen, this doll has at her waist a tiny chatelaine with an imitation pendant watch. (66cm)

38 Details of late nineteenth-century novelty baby doll with triple-faced bisque head which turns on a central wooden peg within a cardboard 'bonnet'. It has ball-jointed wooden arms and legs, and a mechanism in its torso, possibly to make it cry. (44cm)

39 Baby doll with poured-wax head and limbs, brown hair and glass eyes; possibly made in the early 1870s by the Pierotti family. Some of this doll's clothes are of a later date, suggesting two generations of owners. (44.5cm)

37

39

40 Bavarian celluloid baby doll of
1910–20; jointed at hips and
shoulders, with the impressed
turtle trademark of 'Rheinische
Gummi und Celluloid Fabrik Co'.
The doll wears a flannelette binder
and nappy and rests on a
lace-trimmed pillow
and mattress.
(25cm)

41 German walking doll of 1910–12 by Simon & Halbig, wearing
a dress, coat and bonnet of dark green corduroy and cream braid.
Her bisque head turns as she walks and her eyes are weighted to move
from side to side. (55cm)

42 Bisque-headed doll of 1910–20 by Armand Marseille of Germany;
with weighted, sleeping eyes and ball-jointed limbs of wood and
composition. She wears a turquoise velveteen coat and bonnet over her
dress of white broderie anglaise. (52cm)

43 Bisque-headed doll of 1895–1905, with kid body and bisque lower arms. She wears a turquoise velvet outfit; the remainder of her extensive wardrobe has its own miniature trunk. (48cm)

44 Painted bisque-headed doll of 1860–80, wearing the uniform of the London Shoe Black Societies, founded in 1851 by the philanthropist John McGregor to employ homeless boys. (9.5cm)

Inside back cover (right)

Faces of dolls from 1750–1910:

Top row left to right	1	poured wax, 1750–60;
	2	carved wood, 1780–85;
	3	carved wood, 1832–33;
	4	poured wax, 1820–40;
Second row	5	papier-mâché, 1831–36,
	6	poured wax, 1845–50;
	7	poured wax, 1863–65;
	8	glazed porcelain, 1860–70;
Third row	9	glazed and unglazed porcelain, 1865–67;
	10	poured wax, 1865–70;
	11	poured wax, 1865–70;
	12	bisque, 1865–70;
Bottom row	13	solid wax, 1901–2;
	14	bisque, 1910–15;
	15	bisque, 1900–10;
	16	bisque, 1910–15

43

ACKNOWLEDGEMENTS

This booklet was published to accompany 'Hello Dolly' an exhibition drawn from the Museum's doll collection, November 1986 to April 1987. The Museum of London acknowledges with appreciation the advice of Mary Hillier, financial assistance for the exhibition from the Friends of Fashion, the National Magazine Company, and Sotheby's, and additional conservation by Plowden and Smith Limited through the Area Museums Service for South East England, the Textile Conservation Centre, and Danielle Bosworth.

SELECTED READING

COLEMAN, D S, E A & E J Collector's Encyclopedia of Dolls, London (1968)
COLEMAN, D S, E A & E J The Collector's Book of Dolls' Clothes, London (1976)
GOODFELLOW, C C Understanding Dolls, Woodbridge (1983)
HILLIER, M The History of Wax Dolls, London (1985)
MANSELL, C Collector's Guide to British Dolls since 1920, London (1983)
STANILAND, K Fashion in Miniature, Manchester (1970)
TARNOWSKA, M Fashion Dolls, London (1986)

44

BY THE SAME AUTHOR
ALL PUBLISHED BY HOUSE OF STRATUS

GW00599398

The Wonderful Visit

The Wonderful Visit

H G WELLS

HOUSE OF
STRATUS

This edition published in 2002 by House of Stratus, an imprint of
House of Stratus Ltd, Thirsk Industrial Park, York Road, Thirsk,
North Yorkshire, YO7 3BX, UK.
Also at: House of Stratus Inc., 2 Neptune Road, Poughkeepsie, NY 12601, USA.

www.houseofstratus.com

Typeset, printed and bound by House of Stratus.

A catalogue record for this book is available from the British Library
and The Library of Congress.

ISBN 0-7551-0429-3

To the Memory of My Dear Friend,
Walter Low

CONTENTS

CHAPTER ONE

The Night of the Strange Bird

On the Night of the Strange Bird, many people at Sidderton (and some nearer) saw a Glare on the Sidderford moor. But no one in Sidderford saw it, for most of Sidderford was abed.

All day the wind had been rising, so that the larks on the moor chirruped fitfully near the ground, or rose only to be driven like leaves before the wind. The sun set in a bloody welter of clouds, and the moon was hidden. The glare, they say, was golden like a beam shining out of the sky, not a uniform blaze, but broken all over by curving flashes like the waving of swords. It lasted but a moment and left the night dark and obscure. There were letters about it in *Nature*, and a rough drawing that no one thought very like. (You may see it for yourself – the drawing that was unlike the glare – on page 42 of Vol. cclx of that publication.)

None in Sidderford saw the light, but Annie, Hooker Durgan's wife, was lying awake, and she saw the reflection of it – a flickering tongue of gold – dancing on the wall.

She, too, was one of those who heard the sound. The others who heard the sound were Lumpy Durgan, the half-wit, and Amory's mother. They said it was a sound like children singing

1

and a throbbing of harp strings, carried on a rush of notes like that which sometimes comes from an organ. It began and ended like the opening and shutting of a door, and before and after they heard nothing but the night wind howling over the moor and the noise of the caves under Sidderford cliff. Amory's mother said she wanted to cry when she heard it, but Lumpy was only sorry he could hear no more.

That is as much as anyone can tell you of the glare upon Sidderford Moor and the alleged music therewith. And whether these had any real connection with the Strange Bird whose history follows, is more than I can say. But I set it down here for reasons that will be more apparent as the story proceeds.

CHAPTER TWO

The Coming of the Strange Bird

Sandy Bright was coming down the road from Spinner's carrying a side of bacon he had taken in exchange for a clock. He saw nothing of the light but he heard and saw the Strange Bird. He suddenly heard a flapping and a voice like a woman wailing, and being a nervous man and all alone, he was alarmed forthwith, and turning (all a-tremble) saw something large and black against the dim darkness of the cedars up the hill. It seemed to be coming right down upon him, and incontinently he dropped his bacon and set off running, only to fall headlong.

He tried in vain – such was his state of mind – to remember the beginning of the Lord's Prayer. The strange bird flapped over him, something larger than himself, with a vast spread of wings, and, as he thought, black. He screamed and gave himself up for lost. Then it went past him, sailing down the hill, and, soaring over the vicarage, vanished into the hazy valley towards Sidderford.

And Sandy Bright lay upon his stomach there, for ever so long, staring into the darkness after the strange bird. At last he got upon his knees and began to thank Heaven for his merciful deliverance, with his eyes downhill. He went on down into the village, talking aloud and confessing his sins as he went, lest the strange bird should come back. All who heard him thought him drunk. But from that night he was a changed man, and had done with drunkenness and defrauding the revenue by selling silver ornaments without a licence. And the side of bacon lay upon the hillside until the tallyman from Portburdock found it in the morning.

The next who saw the Strange Bird was a solicitor's clerk at Iping Hanger, who was climbing the hill before breakfast, to see the sunrise. Save for a few dissolving wisps of cloud the sky had been blown clear in the night. At first he thought it was an eagle he saw. It was near the zenith, and incredibly remote, a mere bright speck above the pink cirri, and it seemed as if it fluttered and beat itself against the sky, as an imprisoned swallow might do against a window pane. Then down it came into the shadow of the earth, sweeping in a great curve towards Portburdock and round over the Hanger, and so vanishing behind the woods of Siddermorton Park. It seemed larger than a man. Just before it was hidden, the light of the rising sun smote over the edge of the downs and touched its wings, and they flashed with the brightness of flames and the colour of precious stones, and so passed, leaving the witness agape.

A ploughman going to his work, along under the stone wall of Siddermorton Park, saw the Strange Bird flash over him for a moment and vanish among the hazy interstices of the beech trees. But he saw little of the colour of the wings, witnessing only that its legs, which were long, seemed pink and bare like naked flesh, and its body mottled white. It smote like an arrow through the air and was gone.

These were the first three eye-witnesses of the Strange Bird.

Now in these days one does not cower before the devil and one's own sinfulness, or see strange iridiscent wings in the light of dawn, and say nothing of it afterwards. The young solicitor's clerk told his mother and sisters at breakfast, and, afterwards, on his way to the office at Portburdock, spoke of it to the blacksmith of Hammerpond, and spent the morning with his fellow clerks marvelling instead of copying deeds. And Sandy Bright went to talk the matter over with Mr Jekyll, the "Primitive" minister, and the ploughman told old Hugh and afterwards the vicar of Siddermorton.

"They are not an imaginative race about here," said the Vicar of Siddermorton, "I wonder how much of that was true. Barring that he thinks the wings were brown it sounds uncommonly like a Flamingo."

CHAPTER THREE

The Hunting of the Strange Bird

T he Vicar of Siddermorton (which is nine miles inland from Siddermouth as the crow flies) was an ornithologist. Some such pursuit, botany, antiquity, folklore, is almost inevitable for a single man in his position. He was given to geometry also, propounding occasionally impossible problems in the *Educational Times*, but ornithology was his *forte*. He had already added two visitors to the list of occasional British birds. His name was well-known in the columns of the *Zoologist* (I am afraid it may be forgotten by now, for the world moves apace). And on the day after the coming of the Strange Bird, came first one and then another to confirm the ploughman's story and tell him, not that it had any connection, of the Glare upon Sidderford moor.

Now, the Vicar of Siddermorton had two rivals in his scientific pursuits; Gully of Sidderton, who had actually seen the glare, and who it was sent the drawing to *Nature*, and Borland the natural history dealer, who kept the marine laboratory at Portburdock. Borland, the Vicar thought, should have stuck to his copepods, but instead he kept a taxidermist, and took advantage of his littoral position to pick up rare sea birds. It was evident to anyone who knew anything of collecting that both these men would be scouring the country after the strange visitant, before twenty-four hours were out.

The Vicar's eye rested on the back of *Saunders' British Birds*, for he was in his study at the time. Already in two places there was entered: "the only known British specimen was secured by the Rev. K Hilyer, Vicar of Siddermorton." A third such entry. He doubted if any other collector had that.

He looked at his watch – *two*. He had just lunched, and usually he "rested" in the afternoon. He knew it would make him feel very disagreeable if he went out into the hot sunshine – both on the top of his head and generally. Yet Gully perhaps was out, prowling observant. Suppose it was something very good and Gully got it!

His gun stood in the corner. (The thing had iridiscent wings and pink legs! The chromatic conflict was certainly exceedingly stimulating.) He took his gun.

He would have gone out by the glass doors and verandah, and down the garden into the hill road, in order to avoid his housekeeper's eye. He knew his gun expeditions were not approved of. But advancing towards him up the garden, he saw the curate's wife and her two daughters, carrying tennis rackets. His curate's wife was a young woman of immense will, who used to play tennis on his lawn, and cut his roses, differ from him on doctrinal points, and criticise his personal behaviour all over the parish. He went in abject fear of her, was always trying to propitiate her. But so far he had clung to his ornithology...

However, he went out by the front door.

If it were not for collectors England would be full, so to speak, of rare birds and wonderful butterflies, strange flowers and a thousand interesting things. But happily the collector prevents all that, either killing with his own hands or, by buying extravagantly, procuring people of the lower classes to kill such eccentricities as appear. It makes work for people, even though Acts of Parliament interfere. In this way, for instance, he is killing off the chough in Cornwall, the Bath white butterfly, the Queen of Spain Fritillary; and can plume himself upon the extermination of the Great Auk, and a hundred other rare birds and plants and insects. All that is the work of the collector and his glory alone. In the name of Science. And this is right and as it should be; eccentricity, in fact, is immorality – think over it again if you do not think so now – just as eccentricity in one's way of thinking is madness (I defy you to find another definition that will fit all the cases of either); and if a species is rare it follows that it is not Fitted to Survive. The collector is after all merely like the foot soldier in the days of heavy armour – he leaves the combatants alone and cuts the throats of those who are overthrown. So one may go through England from end to end in the summer time and see only eight or ten commonplace wild flowers, and the commoner butterflies, and a dozen or so common birds, and never be offended by any breach of the monotony, any splash of strange blossom or flutter of unknown wing. All the rest have been "collected" years ago. For which cause we should all love Collectors, and bear in mind what we owe them when their little collections are displayed. These camphorated little drawers of theirs, their glass cases and blotting-paper books, are the graves of the Rare and the Beautiful, the symbols of the Triumph of Leisure (morally spent) over the Delights of Life. (All of which, as you very properly remark, has nothing whatever to do with the Strange Bird.)

3

There is a place on the moor where the black water shines among the succulent moss, and the hairy sundew, eater of careless insects, spreads its red-stained hungry hands to the God who gives his creatures – one to feed another. On a ridge thereby grow birches with a silvery bark, and the soft green of the larch mingles with the dark green fir. Thither through the honey humming heather came the Vicar, in the heat of the day, carrying a gun under his arm, a gun loaded with swanshot for the Strange Bird. And over his disengaged hand he carried a pocket handkerchief wherewith, ever and again, he wiped his beady face.

He went by and on past the big pond and the pool full of brown leaves where the Sidder arises, and so by the road (which is at first sandy and then chalky) to the little gate that goes into the park. There are seven steps up to the gate and on the further side six down again – lest the deer escape – so that when the Vicar stood in the gateway his head was ten feet or more above the ground. And looking where a tumult of bracken fronds filled the hollow between two groups of beech, his eye caught something parti-coloured that wavered and went. Suddenly his face gleamed and his muscles grew tense; he ducked his head, clutched his gun with both hands, and stood still. Then watching keenly, he came on down the steps into the park, and still holding his gun in both hands, crept rather than walked towards the jungle of bracken.

Nothing stirred, and he almost feared that his eyes had played him false, until he reached the ferns and had gone rustling breast high into them. Then suddenly rose something full of wavering colours, twenty yards or less in front of his face, and beating the air. In another moment it had fluttered above the bracken and spread its pinions wide. He saw what it was, his heart was in his mouth, and he fired out of pure surprise and habit.

There was a scream of superhuman agony, the wings beat the air twice, and the victim came slanting swiftly downward and struck the ground – a struggling heap of writhing body, broken wing and flying bloodstained plumes – upon the turfy slope behind.

The Vicar stood aghast, with his smoking gun in his hand. It was no bird at all, but a youth with an extremely beautiful face, clad in a robe of saffron and with iridescent wings, across whose pinions great waves of colour, flushes of purple and crimson, golden green and intense blue, pursued one another as he writhed in his agony. Never had the Vicar seen such gorgeous floods of colour, not stained glass windows, not the wings of butterflies, not even the glories of crystals seen between prisms, no colours on earth could compare with them. Twice the Angel raised himself, only to fall over sideways again. Then the beating of the wings diminished, the terrified face grew pale, the floods of colour abated, and suddenly with a sob he lay prone, and the changing hues of the broken wings faded swiftly into one uniform dull grey hue.

"Oh! *what* has happened to me?" cried the Angel (for such it was), shuddering violently, hands outstretched and clutching the ground, and then lying still.

"Dear me!" said the Vicar. "I had no idea." He came forward cautiously. "Excuse me," he said, "I am afraid I have shot you."

It was the obvious remark.

The Angel seemed to become aware of his presence for the first time. He raised himself by one hand, his brown eyes stared into the Vicar's. Then, with a gasp, and biting his nether lip, he struggled into a sitting position and surveyed the Vicar from top to toe.

"A man!" said the Angel, clasping his forehead; "a man in the maddest black clothes and without a feather upon him. Then I was not deceived. I am indeed in the Land of Dreams!"

CHAPTER FOUR

The Vicar and the Angel

Now there are some things frankly impossible. The weakest intellect will admit this situation is impossible. The *Athenaeum* will probably say as much should it venture to review this. Sun-bespattered ferns, spreading beech trees, the Vicar and the gun are acceptable enough. But this Angel is a different matter. Plain sensible people will scarcely go on with such an extravagant book. And the Vicar fully appreciated this impossibility. But he lacked decision. Consequently he went on with it, as you shall immediately hear. He was hot, it was after dinner, he was in no mood for mental subtleties. The Angel had him at a disadvantage, and further distracted him from the main issue by irrelevant iridescence and a violent fluttering. For the moment it never occurred to the Vicar to ask whether the Angel was possible or not. He accepted him in the confusion of the moment, and the mischief was done. Put yourself in his place, my dear *Athenaeum*. You go out shooting. You hit something. That alone would disconcert you. You find you have hit an Angel, and he writhes about for a minute and then sits up and addresses you. He makes no apology for his own impossibility. Indeed, he carries the charge clean into your camp. "A man!" he says, pointing. "A man in the maddest black clothes and without a feather upon him. Then I was not deceived. I am indeed in the Land of Dreams!" You must answer him. Unless you take to your heels. Or blow his brains out with your second barrel as an escape from the controversy.

"The Land of Dreams! Pardon me if I suggest you have just come out of it," was the Vicar's remark.

"How can that be?" said the Angel.

"Your wing," said the Vicar, "is bleeding. Before we talk, may I have the pleasure – the melancholy pleasure – of tying it up? I am really most sincerely sorry…" The Angel put his hand behind his back and winced.

The Vicar assisted his victim to stand up. The Angel turned gravely and the Vicar, with numberless insignificant panting parentheses, carefully examined the injured wings. (They articulated, he observed with interest, to a kind of second glenoid on the outer and upper edge of the shoulder blade. The left wing had suffered little except the loss of some of the primary wing-quills, and a shot or so in the *ala spuria*, but the humerus bone of the right was evidently smashed.) The Vicar stanched the bleeding as well as he could and tied up the bone with his pocket handkerchief and the neck wrap his housekeeper made him carry in all weathers.

"I'm afraid you will not be able to fly for some time," said he, feeling the bone.

"I don't like this new sensation," said the Angel.

"The Pain when I feel your bone?"

"The *what?*" said the Angel.

"The Pain."

14

" 'Pain' – you call it. No, I certainly don't like the Pain. Do you have much of this Pain in the Land of Dreams?"

"A very fair share," said the Vicar. "Is it new to you?"

"Quite," said the Angel. "I don't like it."

"How curious!" said the Vicar, and bit at the end of a strip of linen to tie a knot. "I think this bandaging must serve for the present," he said. "I've studied ambulance work before, but never the bandaging up of wing wounds. Is your Pain any better?"

"It glows now instead of flashing," said the Angel.

"I am afraid you will find it glow for some time," said the Vicar, still intent on the wound.

The Angel gave a shrug of the wing and turned round to look at the Vicar again. He had been trying to keep an eye on the Vicar over his shoulder during all their interview. He looked at him from top to toe with raised eyebrows and a growing smile on his beautiful soft-featured face. "It seems so odd," he said with a sweet little laugh, "to be talking to a Man!"

"Do you know," said the Vicar, "now that I come to think of it, it is equally odd to me that I should be talking to an Angel. I am a somewhat matter-of-fact person. A Vicar has to be. Angels I have always regarded as – artistic conceptions – "

"Exactly what we think of men."

"But surely you have seen so many men – "

"Never before today. In pictures and books, times enough of course. But I have seen several since the sunrise, solid real men, besides a horse or so – those Unicorn things you know, without horns – and quite a number of those grotesque knobby things called 'cows.' I was naturally a little frightened at so many mythical monsters, and came to hide here until it was dark. I suppose it will be dark again presently like it was at first. *Phew!* This Pain of yours is poor fun. I hope I shall wake up directly."

"I don't understand quite," said the Vicar, knitting his brows and tapping his forehead with his flat hand. "Mythical monster!" The worst thing he had been called for years hitherto was a 'mediaeval anachronism' (by an advocate of Disestablishment). "Do I understand that you consider me as – as something in a dream?"

"Of course," said the Angel smiling.

"And this world about me, these rugged trees and spreading fronds – "

"Is all so *very* dream-like," said the Angel. "Just exactly what one dreams of – or artists imagine."

"You have artists then among the Angels?"

"All kinds of artists, Angels with wonderful imaginations, who invent men and cows and eagles and a thousand impossible creatures."

"Impossible creatures!" said the Vicar.

"Impossible creatures," said the Angel. "Myths."

"But I'm real!" said the Vicar. "I assure you I'm real."

The Angel shrugged his wings and winced and smiled. "I can always tell when I am dreaming," he said.

"*You* – dreaming," said the Vicar. He looked round him. "*You* dreaming!" he repeated. His mind worked diffusely.

He held out his hand with all his fingers moving. "I have it!" he said. "I begin to see." A really brilliant idea was dawning upon his mind. He had not studied mathematics at Cambridge for nothing, after all. "Tell me please. Some animals of *your* world...of the Real World, real animals you know."

"Real animals!" said the Angel smiling. "Why – there's Griffins and Dragons – and Jabberwocks – and Cherubim – and Sphinxes – and the Hippogriff – and Mermaids – and Satyrs – and…"

"Thank you," said the Vicar as the Angel appeared to be warming to his work; "thank you. That is *quite* enough. I begin to understand."

He paused for a moment, his face pursed up. "Yes… I begin to see it."

"See what?" asked the Angel.

"The Griffins and Satyrs and so forth. It's as clear…"

"I don't see them," said the Angel.

"No, the whole point is they are not to be seen in this world. But our men with imaginations have told us all about them, you know. And even I at times…there are places in this village where you must simply take what they set before you, or give offence – I, I say, have seen in my dreams Jabberwocks, Bogle brutes, Mandrakes… From our point of view, you know, they are Dream Creatures…"

"Dream Creatures!" said the Angel. "How singular! This is a very curious dream. A kind of topsy-turvey one. You call men real and angels a myth. It almost makes one think that in some odd way there must be two worlds as it were…"

"At least Two," said the Vicar.

"Lying somewhere close together, and yet scarcely suspecting…"

"As near as page to page of a book."

"Penetrating each other, living each its own life. This is really a delicious dream!"

"And never dreaming of each other."

17

"Except when people go a-dreaming!"

"Yes," said the Angel thoughtfully. "It must be something of the sort. And that reminds me. Sometimes when I have been dropping asleep, or drowsing under the noon-tide sun, I have seen strange corrugated faces just like yours, going by me, and trees with green leaves upon them, and such queer uneven ground as this... It must be so. I have fallen into another world."

"Sometimes," began the Vicar, "at bedtime, when I have been just on the edge of consciousness, I have seen faces as beautiful as yours, and the strange dazzling vistas of a wonderful scene, that flowed past me, winged shapes soaring over it, and wonderful – sometimes terrible – forms going to and fro. I have even heard sweet music too in my ears... It may be that as we withdraw our attention from the world of sense, the pressing world about us, as we pass into the twilight of repose, other worlds... Just as we see the stars, those other worlds in space, when the glare of day recedes... And the artistic dreamers who see such things most clearly..."

They looked at one another.

"And in some incomprehensible manner I have fallen into this world of yours out of my own!" said the Angel, "into the world of my dreams, grown real."

He looked about him. "Into the world of my dreams."

"It is confusing," said the Vicar. "It almost makes one think there may be (ahem) Four Dimensions after all. In which case, of course," he went on hurriedly – for he loved geometrical speculations and took a certain pride in his knowledge of them – "there may be any number of three-dimensional universes packed side by side, and all dimly dreaming of one another. There may be world upon world, universe upon universe. It's perfectly possible. There's nothing so incredible as the absolutely possible. But I wonder how you came to fall out of your world into mine…"

"Dear me!" said the Angel; "There's deer and a stag! Just as they draw them on the coats of arms. How grotesque it all seems! Can I really be awake?"

He rubbed his knuckles into his eyes.

The half-dozen of dappled deer came in Indian file obliquely through the trees and halted, watching. "It's no dream – I am really a solid concrete Angel, in Dream Land," said the Angel. He laughed. The Vicar stood surveying him. The Reverend gentleman was pulling his mouth askew after a habit he had, and slowly stroking his chin. He was asking himself whether he too was not in the Land of Dreams.

2

Now in the land of the Angels, so the Vicar learnt in the course of many conversations, there is neither pain nor trouble nor death, marrying nor giving in marriage, birth nor forgetting. Only at times new things begin. It is a land without hill or dale, a wonderfully level land, glittering with strange buildings, with incessant sunlight or full moon, and with incessant breezes blowing through the Aeolian traceries of the trees. It is Wonderland, with glittering seas hanging in the sky, across which strange fleets go sailing, none know whither. There the flowers glow in Heaven and the stars shine about one's feet and the breath of life is a delight. The land goes on for ever – there is no solar system nor interstellar space such as there is in our universe – and the air goes upward past the sun into the uttermost abyss of their sky. And there is nothing but Beauty there – all the beauty in our art is but feeble rendering of faint glimpses of that wonderful world, and our composers, our original composers, are those who hear, however faintly, the dust of melody that drives before its winds. And the Angels, and wonderful monsters of bronze and marble and living fire, go to and fro therein.

It is a land of Law – for whatever is, is under the law – but its laws all, in some strange way, differ from ours. Their geometry is different because their space has a curve in it so that all their planes are cylinders; and their law of Gravitation is not according to the law of inverse squares, and there are four-and-twenty primary colours instead of only three. Most of the fantastic things of our science are commonplaces there, and all our earthly science would seem to them the maddest dreaming. There are no flowers upon their plants, for instance, but jets of coloured fire. That, of course, will seem mere nonsense to you because you do not understand Most of what the Angel told the Vicar, indeed the Vicar could not realise, because his own experiences, being only of this world of matter, warred against his understanding. It was too strange to imagine.

What had jolted these twin universes together so that the Angel had fallen suddenly into Sidderford, neither the Angel nor the Vicar could tell. Nor for the matter of that could the author of this story. The author is concerned with the facts of the case, and has neither the desire nor the confidence to explain them. Explanations are the fallacy of a scientific age. And the cardinal fact of the case is this, that out in Siddermorton Park, with the glory of some wonderful world where there is neither sorrow nor sighing, still clinging to him, on the 4th of August 1895, stood an Angel, bright and beautiful, talking to the Vicar of Siddermorton about the plurality of worlds. The author will swear to the Angel, if need be; and there he draws the line.

3

"I have," said the Angel, "a most unusual feeling – here. Have had since sunrise. I don't remember ever having any feeling – here before."

"Not pain, I hope," said the Vicar.

"Oh no! It is quite different from that – a kind of vacuous feeling."

"The atmospheric pressure, perhaps, is a little different," the Vicar began, feeling his chin.

"And do you know, I have also the most curious sensations in my mouth – almost as if – it's so absurd! – as if I wanted to stuff things into it."

"Bless me!" said the Vicar. "Of course! You're hungry!"

"Hungry!" said the Angel. "What's that?"

"Don't you eat?"

"Eat! The word's quite new to me."

"Put food into your mouth, you know. One has to here. You will soon learn. If you don't, you get thin and miserable, and suffer a great deal – *pain*, you know – and finally you die."

"Die!" said the Angel. "That's another strange word!"

"It's not strange here. It means leaving off, you know," said the Vicar.

"We never leave off," said the Angel.

"You don't know what may happen to you in this world," said the Vicar, thinking him over. "Possibly if you are feeling hungry, and can feel pain and have your wings broken, you may even have to die before you get out of it again. At any rate you had better try eating. For my own part – ahem! – there are many more disagreeable things."

"I suppose I *had* better Eat," said the Angel. "If it's not too difficult. I don't like this 'Pain' of yours, and I don't like this 'Hungry.' If your 'Die' is anything like it, I would prefer to Eat. What a very odd world this is!"

"To Die," said the Vicar, "is generally considered worse than either pain or hunger... It depends."

"You must explain all that to me later," said the Angel. "Unless I wake up. At present, please show me how to eat. If you will. I feel a kind of urgency..."

"Pardon me," said the Vicar, and offered an elbow. "If I may have the pleasure of entertaining you. My house lies yonder – not a couple of miles from here."

"*Your* House!" said the Angel a little puzzled; but he took the Vicar's arm affectionately, and the two, conversing as they went, waded slowly through the luxuriant bracken, sun mottled under the trees, and on over the stile in the park palings, and so across the bee-swarming heather for a mile or more, down the hillside, home.

You would have been charmed at the couple could you have seen them. The Angel, slight of figure, scarcely five feet high, and with a beautiful, almost effeminate face, such as an Italian old Master might have painted. (Indeed, there is one in the National Gallery [*Tobias and the Angel*, by some artist unknown] not at all unlike him so far as face and spirit go.) He was robed simply in a purple-wrought saffron blouse, bare kneed and bare-footed, with his wings (broken now, and a leaden grey) folded behind him. The Vicar was a short, rather stout figure, rubicund, red-haired, clean-shaven, and with bright ruddy brown eyes. He wore a piebald straw hat with a black ribbon, a very neat white tie, and a fine gold watch-chain. He was so greatly interested in his companion that it only occurred to him when he was in sight of the Vicarage that he had left his gun lying just where he had dropped it amongst the bracken.

He was rejoiced to hear that the pain of the bandaged wing fell rapidly in intensity.

CHAPTER FIVE

Parenthesis on Angels

L et us be plain. The Angel of this story is the Angel of Art, not the Angel that one must be irreverent to touch – neither the Angel of religious feeling nor the Angel of popular belief. The last we all know. She is alone among the angelic hosts in being distinctly feminine: she wears a robe of immaculate, unmitigated white with sleeves, is fair, with long golden tresses, and has eyes of the blue of Heaven. Just a pure woman she is, pure maiden or pure matron, in her *robe de nuit*, and with wings attached to her shoulder blades. Her callings are domestic and sympathetic, she watches over a cradle or assists a sister soul heavenward. Often she bears a palm leaf, but one would not be surprised if one met her carrying a warming-pan softly to some poor chilly sinner. She it was who came down in a bevy to Marguerite in prison, in the amended last scene in *Faust* at the Lyceum, and the interesting and improving little children that are to die young, have visions of such angels in the novels of Mrs Henry Wood. This white womanliness with her indescribable charm of lavender-like holiness, her aroma of clean, methodical lives, is, it would seem after all, a purely Teutonic invention. Latin thought knows her not; the old masters have none of her. She is of a piece with that gentle innocent ladylike school of art whereof the greatest triumph is "a lump in one's throat," and where wit and passion, scorn and pomp, have no place. The white angel was made in Germany, in the land of blonde women and the domestic sentiments. She comes to us cool and worshipful, pure and tranquil, as silently soothing as the breadth and calmness of the starlit sky, which also is so unspeakably dear to the Teutonic soul... We do her reverence. And to the angels of the Hebrews, those spirits of power and mystery, to Raphael, Zadkiel, and Michael, of whom only Watts has caught the shadow, of whom only Blake has seen the splendour, to them too, do we do reverence.

But this Angel the Vicar shot is, we say, no such angel at all, but the Angel of Italian art, polychromatic and gay. He comes from the land of beautiful dreams and not from any holier place. At best he is a popish creature. Bear patiently, therefore, with his scattered remiges, and be not hasty with your charge of irreverence before the story is read.

CHAPTER SIX

At the Vicarage

The Curate's wife and her two daughters and Mrs Jehoram were still playing at tennis on the lawn behind the Vicar's study, playing keenly and talking in gasps about paper patterns for blouses. But the Vicar forgot and came in that way.

They saw the Vicar's hat above the rhododendrons, and a bare curly head beside him. "I must ask him about Susan Wiggin," said the Curate's wife. She was about to serve, and stood with a racket in one hand and a ball between the fingers of the other. "*He* really ought to have gone to see her – being the Vicar. Not George. I – *Ah*!"

For the two figures suddenly turned the corner and were visible. The Vicar, arm in arm with –

You see, it came on the Curate's wife suddenly. The Angel's face being towards her she saw nothing of the wings. Only a face of unearthly beauty in a halo of chestnut hair, and a graceful figure clothed in a saffron garment that barely reached the knees. The thought of those knees flashed upon the Vicar at once. He too was horrorstruck. So were the two girls and Mrs Jehoram. All horrorstruck. The Angel stared in astonishment at the

27

horrorstruck group. You see, he had never seen anyone horrorstruck before.

"MIS–ter Hillyer!" said the Curate's wife. "This is *too* much!" She stood speechless for a moment. "*Oh!*"

She swept round upon the rigid girls. "Come!" The Vicar opened and shut his voiceless mouth. The world hummed and spun about him. There was a whirling of zephyr skirts, four impassioned faces sweeping towards the open door of the passage that ran through the vicarage. He felt his position went with them.

"Mrs Mendham," said the Vicar, stepping forward. "Mrs Mendham. You don't understand – "

"*Oh!*" they all said again.

One, two, three, four skirts vanished in the doorway. The Vicar staggered halfway across the lawn and stopped, aghast. "This comes," he heard the Curate's wife say, out of the depth of the passage, "of having an unmarried vicar – " The umbrella stand wobbled. The front door of the vicarage slammed like a minute gun. There was silence for a space.

"I might have thought," he said. "She is always so hasty."

He put his hand to his chin – a habit with him. Then turned his face to his companion. The Angel was evidently well bred. He was holding up Mrs Jehoram's sunshade – she had left it on one of the cane chairs – and examining it with extraordinary interest. He opened it. "What a curious little mechanism!" he said. "What can it be for?"

The Vicar did not answer. The angelic costume certainly was – the Vicar knew it was a case for a French phrase – but he could scarcely remember it. He so rarely used French. It was not *de trop*, he knew. Anything but *de trop*. The Angel was *de trop*, but certainly not his costume. Ah! *Sans culotte!*

The Vicar examined his visitor critically – for the first time. "He *will* be difficult to explain," he said to himself softly.

The Angel stuck the sunshade into the turf and went to smell the sweet briar. The sunshine fell upon his brown hair and gave it almost the appearance of a halo. He pricked his finger. "Odd!" he said. "Pain again."

"Yes," said the Vicar, thinking aloud. "He's very beautiful and curious as he is. I should like him best so. But I am afraid I must."

He approached the Angel with a nervous cough.

2

"Those," said the Vicar, "were ladies."

"How grotesque," said the Angel, smiling and smelling the sweet briar. "And such quaint shapes!"

"Possibly," said the Vicar. "Did you, *ahem*, notice how they behaved?"

"They went away. Seemed, indeed, to run away. Frightened? I, of course, was frightened at things without wings. I hope – they were not frightened at my wings?"

"At your appearance generally," said the Vicar, glancing involuntarily at the pink feet.

"Dear me! It never occurred to me. I suppose I seemed as odd to them as you did to me." He glanced down. "And my feet. *You* have hoofs like a hippogriff."

"Boots," corrected the Vicar.

"Boots, you call them! But anyhow, I am sorry I alarmed – "

29

"You see," said the Vicar, stroking his chin, "our ladies, *ahem*, have peculiar views – rather inartistic views – about, *ahem*, clothing. Dressed as you are, I am afraid, I am really afraid that – beautiful as your costume certainly is – you will find yourself somewhat, *ahem*, somewhat isolated in society. We have a little proverb, 'When in Rome, *ahem*, one must do as the Romans do.' I can assure you that, assuming you are desirous to *ahem*, associate with us – during your involuntary stay – "

The Angel retreated a step or so as the Vicar came nearer and nearer in his attempt to be diplomatic and confidential. The beautiful face grew perplexed. "I don't quite understand. Why do you keep making these noises in your throat? Is it Die or Eat, or any of those..."

"As your host," interrupted the Vicar, and stopped.

"As my host," said the Angel.

"*Would* you object, pending more permanent arrangements, to invest yourself, *ahem*, in a suit, an entirely new suit I may say, like this I have on?"

"Oh!" said the Angel. He retreated so as to take in the Vicar from top to toe. "Wear clothes like yours!" he said. He was puzzled but amused. His eyes grew round and bright, his mouth puckered at the corners.

"Delightful!" he said, clapping his hands together. "What a mad, quaint dream this is! Where are they?" He caught at the neck of the saffron robe.

"Indoors!" said the Vicar. "This way. We will change – indoors!"

3

So the Angel was invested in a pair of nether garments of the Vicar's, a shirt, ripped down the back (to accommodate the wings), socks, shoes – the Vicar's dress shoes – collar, tie, and light overcoat. But putting on the latter was painful, and reminded the Vicar that the bandaging was temporary. "I will ring for tea at once, and send Grummet down for Crump," said the Vicar. "And dinner shall be earlier." While the Vicar shouted his orders on the landing rails, the Angel surveyed himself in the cheval glass with immense delight. If he was a stranger to pain, he was evidently no stranger – thanks perhaps to dreaming – to the pleasure of incongruity.

They had tea in the drawing-room. The Angel sat on the music stool (music stool because of his wings). At first he wanted to lie on the hearthrug. He looked much less radiant in the Vicar's clothes, than he had done upon the moor when dressed in saffron. His face shone still, the colour of his hair and cheeks was strangely bright, and there was a superhuman light in his eyes, but his wings under the overcoat gave him the appearance of a hunchback. The garments, indeed, made quite a terrestrial thing of him, the trousers were puckered transversely, and the shoes a size or so too large.

He was charmingly affable and quite ignorant of the most elementary facts of civilisation. Eating came without much difficulty, and the Vicar had an entertaining time teaching him how to take tea. "What a mess it is! What a dear grotesque ugly world you live in!" said the Angel. "Fancy stuffing things into your mouth! We use our mouths just to talk and sing with. Our world, you know, is almost incurably beautiful. We get so very little ugliness, that I find all this...delightful."

Mrs Hinijer, the Vicar's housekeeper, looked at the Angel suspiciously when she brought in the tea. She thought him rather a "queer customer." What she would have thought had she seen him in saffron no one can tell.

The Angel shuffled about the room with his cup of tea in one hand, and the bread and butter in the other, and examined the Vicar's furniture. Outside the French windows, the lawn with its array of dahlias and sunflowers glowed in the warm sunlight, and Mrs Jehoram's sunshade stood thereon like a triangle of fire. He thought the Vicar's portrait over the mantel very curious indeed, could not understand what it was there for. "You have yourself round," he said, *apropos* of the portrait, "Why want yourself flat?" and he was vastly amused at the glass fire screen. He found the oak chairs odd – "You're not square, are you?" he said, when the Vicar explained their use. "*We* never double ourselves up. We lie about on the asphodel when we want to rest."

"The chair," said the Vicar, "to tell you the truth, has always puzzled *me*. It dates, I think, from the days when the floors were cold and very dirty. I suppose we have kept up the habit. It's become a kind of instinct with us to sit on chairs. Anyhow, if I went to see one of my parishioners, and suddenly spread myself out on the floor – the natural way of it – I don't know what she would do. It would be all over the parish in no time. Yet it seems the natural method of reposing, to recline. The Greeks and Romans – "

"What is this?" said the Angel abruptly.

"That's a stuffed kingfisher. I killed it."

"Killed it!"

"Shot it," said the Vicar, "with a gun."

"Shot! As you did me?"

"I didn't kill you, you see. Fortunately."

"Is killing making like that?"

"In a way."

"Dear me! And you wanted to make me like that – wanted to put glass eyes in me and string me up in a glass case full of ugly green and brown stuff?"

"You see," began the Vicar, "I scarcely understood – "

"Is that 'die'?" asked the Angel suddenly.

"That is dead; it died."

"Poor little thing. I must eat a lot. But you say you killed it. *Why?*"

"You see," said the Vicar, "I take an interest in birds, and I (*ahem*) collect them. I wanted the specimen – "

The Angel stared at him for a moment with puzzled eyes. "A beautiful bird like that!" he said with a shiver. "Because the fancy took you. You wanted the specimen!"

He thought for a minute. "Do you often kill?" he asked the Vicar.

CHAPTER SEVEN

The Man of Science

Then Doctor Crump arrived. Grummet had met him not a hundred yards from the vicarage gate. He was a large, rather heavy-looking man, with a clean-shaven face and a double chin. He was dressed in a grey morning coat (he always affected grey), with a chequered black and white tie. "What's the trouble?" he said, entering and staring without a shadow of surprise at the Angel's radiant face.

"This – *ahem* – gentleman," said the Vicar, "or – *ah* – Angel" – the Angel bowed – "is suffering from a gunshot wound."

"Gunshot wound!" said Doctor Crump. "In July! May I look at it, Mr – Angel, I think you said?"

"He will probably be able to assuage your pain," said the Vicar. "Let me assist you to remove your coat?"

The Angel turned obediently.

"Spinal curvature?" muttered Doctor Crump quite audibly, walking round behind the Angel. "No! abnormal growth. Hullo! This is odd!" He clutched the left wing. "Curious," he said. "Reduplication of the anterior limb – bifid coracoid. Possible, of course, but I've never seen it before." The angel winced under

35

his hands. "Humerus. Radius and Ulna. All there. Congenital, of course. Humerus broken. Curious integumentary simulation of feathers. Dear me. Almost avian. Probably of considerable interest in comparative anatomy. I never did! – How did this gunshot happen, Mr Angel?"

The Vicar was amazed at the Doctor's matter-of-fact manner.

"Our friend," said the Angel, moving his head at the Vicar.

"Unhappily it is my doing," said the Vicar, stepping forward, explanatory. "I mistook the gentleman – the Angel (*ahem*) – for a large bird – "

"Mistook him for a large bird! What next? Your eyes want seeing to," said Doctor Crump. "I've told you so before." He went on patting and feeling, keeping time with a series of grunts and inarticulate mutterings… "But this is really a very good bit of amateur bandaging," said he. "I think I shall leave it. Curious malformation this is! Don't you find it inconvenient, Mr Angel?"

He suddenly walked round so as to look in the Angel's face.

The Angel thought he referred to the wound. "It is rather," he said.

"If it wasn't for the bones I should say paint with iodine night and morning. Nothing like iodine. You could paint your face flat with it. But the osseous outgrowth, the bones, you know, complicate things. I could saw them off, of course. It's not a thing one should have done in a hurry – "

"Do you mean my wings?" said the Angel in alarm.

"Wings!" said the Doctor. "Eigh? Call 'em wings! Yes – what else should I mean?"

"Saw them off!" said the Angel.

"Don't you think so? It's of course your affair. I am only advising – "

"Saw them off! What a funny creature you are!" said the Angel, beginning to laugh.

"As you will," said the Doctor. He detested people who laughed. "The things are curious," he said, turning to the Vicar. "If inconvenient" – to the Angel. "I never heard of such complete reduplication before – at least among animals. In plants it's common enough. Were you the only one in your family?" He did not wait for a reply. "Partial cases of the fission of limbs are not at all uncommon, of course, Vicar – six-fingered children, calves with six feet, and cats with double toes, you know. May I assist you?" he said, turning to the Angel who was struggling with the coat. "But such a complete reduplication, and so avian, too! It would be much less remarkable if it was simply another pair of arms."

The coat was got on and he and the Angel stared at one another.

"Really," said the Doctor, "one begins to understand how that beautiful myth of the angels arose. You look a little hectic, Mr Angel – feverish. Excessive brilliance is almost worse as a symptom than excessive pallor. Curious your name should be Angel. I must send you a cooling draught, if you should feel thirsty in the night..."

He made a memorandum on his shirt cuff. The Angel watched him thoughtfully, with the dawn of a smile in his eyes.

"One minute, Crump," said the Vicar, taking the Doctor's arm and leading him towards the door.

The Angel's smile grew brighter. He looked down at his black-clad legs. "He positively thinks I am a man!" said the Angel.

"What he makes of the wings beats me altogether. What a queer creature he must be! This is really a most extraordinary Dream!"

2

"That *is* an Angel," whispered the Vicar. "You don't understand."

"*What*?" said the Doctor in a quick, sharp voice. His eyebrows went up and he smiled.

"But the wings?"

"Quite natural, quite…if a little abnormal."

"Are you sure they are natural?"

"My dear fellow, everything that is, is natural. There is nothing unnatural in the world. If I thought there was I should give up practice and go into *Le Grand Chartreuse*. There are abnormal phenomena, of course. And – "

"But the way I came upon him," said the Vicar.

"Yes, tell me where you picked him up," said the Doctor. He sat down on the hall table.

The Vicar began rather hesitatingly – he was not very good at storytelling – with the rumours of a strange great bird. He told the story in clumsy sentences – for, knowing the Bishop as he did, with that awful example always before him he dreaded getting his pulpit style into his daily conversation – and at every third sentence or so, the Doctor made a downward movement of his head – the corners of his mouth tucked away, so to speak – as though he ticked off the phases of the story and so far found it just as it ought to be. "Self-hypnotism," he murmured once.

"I beg your pardon?" said the Vicar.

"Nothing," said the Doctor. "Nothing, I assure you. Go on. This is extremely interesting."

The Vicar told him he went out with his gun.

"*After* lunch, I think you said?" interrupted the Doctor.

"Immediately after," said the Vicar.

"You should not do such things, you know. But go on, please."

He came to the glimpse of the Angel from the gate.

"In the full glare," said the Doctor in parenthesis. "It was seventy-nine in the shade."

When the Vicar had finished, the Doctor pressed his lips together tighter than ever, smiled faintly, and looked significantly into the Vicar's eyes.

"You don't..." began the Vicar, falteringly.

The Doctor shook his head. "Forgive me," he said, putting his hand on the Vicar's arm.

"You go out," he said, "on a hot lunch and on a hot afternoon. Probably over eighty. Your mind, what there is of it, is whirling with avian expectations. I say, 'what there is of it,' because most of your nervous energy is down there, digesting your dinner. A man who has been lying in the bracken stands up before you and you blaze away. Over he goes – and as it happens – as it happens – he has reduplicate forelimbs, one pair being not unlike wings. It's a coincidence certainly. And as for his iridescent colours and so forth – . Have you never had patches of colour swim before your eyes before, on a brilliant sunlight day?... Are you sure they were confined to the wings? Think."

"But he says he *is* an Angel!" said the Vicar, staring out of his little round eyes, his plump hands in his pockets.

"*Ah!*" said the Doctor with his eye on the Vicar. "I expected as much." He paused.

"But don't you think..." began the Vicar.

"That man," said the Doctor in a low, earnest voice, "is a mattoid."

"A what?" said the Vicar.

"A mattoid. An abnormal man. Did you notice the effeminate delicacy of his face? His tendency to quite unmeaning laughter? His neglected hair? Then consider his singular dress..."

The Vicar's hand went up to his chin.

"Marks of mental weakness," said the Doctor. "Many of this type of degenerate show this same disposition to assume some vast mysterious credentials. One will call himself the Prince of Wales, another the Archangel Gabriel, another the Deity even. Ibsen thinks he is a Great Teacher, and Maeterlink a new Shakespeare. I've just been reading all about it – in Nordau. No doubt his odd deformity gave him an idea..."

"But really," began the Vicar.

"No doubt he's slipped away from confinement."

"I do not altogether accept..."

"You will. If not, there's the police, and failing that, advertisement; but, of course, his people may want to hush it up. It's a sad thing in a family..."

"He seems so altogether..."

"Probably you'll hear from his friends in a day or so," said the Doctor, feeling for his watch. "He can't live far from here, I should think. He seems harmless enough. I must come along and see that wing again tomorrow." He slid off the hall table and stood up.

"Those old wives' tales still have their hold on you," he said, patting the Vicar on the shoulder. "But an angel, you know – Ha, ha!"

"I certainly *did* think..." said the Vicar dubiously.

"Weigh the evidence," said the Doctor, still fumbling at his watch. "Weigh the evidence with our instruments of precision. What does it leave you? Splashes of colour, spots of fancy – *muscae volantes.*"

"And yet," said the Vicar, "I could almost swear to the glory on his wings..."

"Think it over," said the Doctor (watch out); "hot afternoon – brilliant sunshine – boiling down on your head... But really I *must* be going. It is a quarter to five. I'll see your – angel (ha, ha!) tomorrow again, if no one has been to fetch him in the meanwhile. Your bandaging was really very good. I flatter *myself* on that score. Our ambulance classes *were* a success you see... Good afternoon."

CHAPTER EIGHT

The Curate

The Vicar opened the door half mechanically to let out Crump, and saw Mendham, his curate, coming up the pathway by the hedge of purple vetch and meadowsweet. At that his hand went up to his chin and his eyes grew perplexed. Suppose he was deceived. The Doctor passed the Curate with a sweep of his hand from his hat brim. Crump was an extraordinarily clever fellow, the Vicar thought, and knew far more of anyone's brain than one did oneself. The Vicar felt that so acutely. It made the coming explanation difficult. Suppose he were to go back into the drawing-room, and find just a tramp asleep on the hearthrug.

Mendham was a cadaverous man with a magnificent beard. He looked, indeed, as though he had run to beard as a mustard plant does to seed. But when he spoke you found he had a voice as well.

"My wife came home in a dreadful state," he brayed out at long range.

"Come in," said the Vicar; "come in. Most remarkable occurrence. Please come in. Come into the study. I'm really dreadfully sorry. But when I explain…"

"And apologise, I hope," brayed the Curate.

43

"And apologise. No, not that way. This way. The study."

"Now what *was* that woman?" said the Curate, turning on the Vicar as the latter closed the study door.

"What woman?"

"Pah!"

"But really!"

"The painted creature in light attire – disgustingly light attire, to speak freely – with whom you were promenading the garden."

"My dear Mendham – that was an Angel!"

"A very pretty Angel?"

"The world is getting so matter-of-fact," said the Vicar.

"The world," roared the Curate, "grows blacker every day. But to find a man in your position, shamelessly, openly…"

"*Bother!*" said the Vicar aside. He rarely swore. "Look here, Mendham, you really misunderstand. I can assure you…"

"Very well," said the Curate. "Explain!" He stood with his lank legs apart, his arms folded, scowling at his Vicar over his big beard.

(Explanations, I repeat, I have always considered the peculiar fallacy of this scientific age.)

The Vicar looked about him helplessly. The world had all gone dull and dead. Had he been dreaming all the afternoon? Was there really an angel in the drawing-room? Or was he the sport of a complicated hallucination?

"Well?" said Mendham, at the end of a minute.

The Vicar's hand fluttered about his chin. "It's such a round-about story," he said.

"No doubt it will be," said Mendham harshly.

The Vicar restrained a movement of impatience.

"I went out to look for a strange bird this afternoon... Do you believe in angels, Mendham, real angels?"

"I'm not here to discuss theology. I am the husband of an insulted woman."

"But I tell you it's not a figure of speech; this *is* an angel, a real angel with wings. He's in the next room now. You do misunderstand me, so..."

"Really, Hilyer – "

"It is true I tell you, Mendham. I swear it is true." The Vicar's voice grew impassioned. "What sin I have done that I should entertain and clothe angelic visitants, I don't know. I only know that – inconvenient as it undoubtedly will be – I have an angel now in the drawing-room, wearing my new suit and finishing his tea. And he's stopping with me, indefinitely, at my invitation. No doubt it was rash of me. But I can't turn him out, you know, because Mrs Mendham – I may be a weakling, but I am still a gentleman."

"Really, Hilyer – "

"I can assure you it is true." There was a note of hysterical desperation in the Vicar's voice. "I fired at him, taking him for a flamingo, and hit him in the wing."

"I thought this was a case for the Bishop. I find it is a case for the Lunacy Commissioners."

"Come and see him, Mendham!"

"But there *are* no angels."

"We teach the people differently," said the Vicar.

"Not as material bodies," said the Curate.

"Anyhow, come and see him."

"I don't want to see your hallucinations," began the Curate.

"I can't explain anything unless you come and see him," said the Vicar. "A man who's more like an angel than anything else in heaven or earth. You simply must see if you wish to understand."

"I don't wish to understand," said the Curate. "I don't wish to lend myself to any imposture. Surely, Hilyer, if this is not an imposition, you can tell me yourself... Flamingo, indeed!"

2

The Angel had finished his tea and was standing looking pensively out of the window. He thought the old church down the valley lit by the light of the setting sun was very beautiful, but he could not understand the serried ranks of tombstones that lay up the hillside beyond. He turned as Mendham and the Vicar came in.

Now Mendham could bully his Vicar cheerfully enough, just as he could bully his congregation; but he was not the sort of man to bully a stranger. He looked at the Angel, and the "strange woman" theory was disposed of. The Angel's beauty was too clearly the beauty of the youth.

"Mr Hilyer tells me," Mendham began, in an almost apologetic tone, "that you – ah – it's so curious – claim to be an Angel."

"*Are* an Angel," said the Vicar.

The Angel bowed.

"Naturally," said Mendham, "we are curious."

"Very," said the Angel. "The blackness and the shape."

"I beg your pardon?" said Mendham.

"The blackness and the flaps," repeated the Angel; "and no wings."

"Precisely," said Mendham, who was altogether at a loss. "We are, of course, curious to know something of how you came into the village in such a peculiar costume."

The Angel looked at the Vicar. The Vicar touched his chin.

"You see," began the Vicar.

"Let *him* explain," said Mendham; "I beg."

"I wanted to suggest," began the Vicar.

"And I don't want you to suggest."

"*Bother!*" said the Vicar.

The Angel looked from one to the other. "Such rugose expressions flit across your faces!" he said.

"You see, Mr – Mr – I don't know your name," said Mendham, with a certain diminution of suavity. "The case stands thus: My wife – four ladies, I might say – are playing lawn tennis, when you suddenly rush out on them, sir; you rush out on them from among the rhododendra in a very defective costume. You and Mr Hilyer.'

"But I – " said the Vicar.

"I know. It was this gentleman's costume was defective. Naturally – it is my place in fact – to demand an explanation." His voice was growing in volume. "And I *must* demand an explanation."

The Angel smiled faintly at his note of anger and his sudden attitude of determination – arms tightly folded.

"I am rather new to the world," the Angel began.

"Nineteen at least," said Mendham. "Old enough to know better. That's a poor excuse."

"May I ask one question first?" said the Angel.

"Well?"

47

"Do you think I am a Man – like yourself? As the chequered man did."

"If you are not a man – "

"One other question. Have you *never* heard of an Angel?"

"I warn you not to try that story upon me," said Mendham, now back at his familiar crescendo.

The Vicar interrupted: "But Mendham – he has wings!"

"*Please* let me talk to him," said Mendham.

"You are so quaint," said the Angel; "you interrupt everything I have to say."

"But what *have* you to say?" said Mendham.

"That I really *am* an Angel..."

"Pshaw!"

"There you go!"

"But tell me, honestly, how you came to be in the shrubbery of Siddermorton Vicarage – in the state in which you were. And in the Vicar's company. Cannot you abandon this ridiculous story of yours?..."

The Angel shrugged his wings. "What *is* the matter with this man?" he said to the Vicar.

"My dear Mendham," said the Vicar, "a few words from me..."

"Surely my question is straightforward enough!"

"But you won't tell me the answer you want, and it's no good my telling you any other."

"*Pshaw!*" said the Curate again. And then turning suddenly on the Vicar, "Where does he come from?"

The Vicar was in a dreadful state of doubt by this time.

"He *says* he is an Angel!" said the Vicar. "Why don't you listen to him?"

"No angel would alarm four ladies..."

"Is *that* what it is all about?" said the Angel.

"Enough cause too, I should think!" said the Curate.

"But I really did not know," said the Angel.

"This is altogether too much!"

"I am sincerely sorry I alarmed these ladies."

"You ought to be. But I see I shall get nothing out of you two." Mendham went towards the door. "I am convinced there is something discreditable at the bottom of this business. Or why not tell a simple straightforward story? I will confess you puzzle me. Why, in this enlightened age, you should tell this fantastic, this far-fetched story of an Angel, altogether beats me. What good *can* it do?..."

"But stop and look at his wings!" said the Vicar. "I can assure you he has wings!"

Mendham had his fingers on the door-handle. "I have seen quite enough," he said. "It may be this is simply a foolish attempt at a hoax, Hilyer."

"But Mendham!" said the Vicar.

The Curate halted in the doorway and looked at the Vicar over his shoulder. The accumulating judgment of months found vent. "I cannot understand, Hilyer, why you are in the Church. For the life of me I cannot. The air is full of Social Movements, of Economic change, the Woman Movement, Rational Dress, The Reunion of Christendom, Socialism, Individualism – all the great and moving Questions of the Hour! Surely, we who follow the Great Reformer... And here you are stuffing birds, and startling ladies with your callous disregard..."

"But Mendham," began the Vicar.

49

The Curate would not hear him. "You shame the Apostles with your levity... But this is only a preliminary enquiry," he said, with a threatening note in his sonorous voice, and so vanished abruptly (with a violent slam) from the room.

3

"Are *all* men so odd as this?" said the Angel.

"I'm in such a difficult position," said the Vicar.

"You see," he said, and stopped, searching his chin for an idea.

"I'm beginning to see," said the Angel.

"They won't believe it."

"I see that."

"They will think I tell lies."

"And?"

"That will be extremely painful to me."

"Painful!... Pain," said the Angel. "I hope not."

The Vicar shook his head. The good report of the village had been the breath of his life, so far. "You see," he said, "it would look so much more plausible if you said you were just a man."

"But I'm not," said the Angel.

"No, you're not," said the Vicar. "So that's no good."

"Nobody here, you know, has ever seen an Angel, or heard of one – except in church. If you had made your *debut* in the chancel – on Sunday – it might have been different. But that's too late now... (*Bother!*) Nobody, absolutely nobody, will believe in you."

"I hope I am not inconveniencing you?"

"Not at all," said the Vicar; "not at all. Only – . Naturally it may be inconvenient if you tell a too incredible story. If I might suggest (*ahem*) – "

"Well?"

"You see, people in the world, being men themselves, will almost certainly regard you as a man. If you say you are not, they will simply say you do not tell the truth. Only exceptional people appreciate the exceptional. When in Rome one must – well, respect Roman prejudices a little – talk Latin. You will find it better – "

"You propose I should feign to become a man?"

"You have my meaning at once."

The Angel stared at the Vicar's hollyhocks and thought.

"Possibly, after all," he said slowly, "I *shall* become a man. I may have been too hasty in saying I was not. You say there are no angels in this world. Who am I to set myself up against your experience? A mere thing of a day – so far as this world goes. If you say there are no angels – clearly I must be something else. I eat – angels do not eat. I *may* be a man already."

"A convenient view, at any rate," said the Vicar.

"If it is convenient to you – "

"It is. And then to account for your presence here."

"*If*," said the Vicar, after a hesitating moment of reflection, "if, for instance, you had been an ordinary man with a weakness for wading, and you had gone wading in the Sidder, and your clothes had been stolen, for instance, and I had come upon you in that position of inconvenience; the explanation I shall have to make to Mrs Mendham – would be shorn at least of the supernatural element. There is such a feeling against the supernatural element nowadays – even in the pulpit. You would hardly believe – "

"It's a pity that was not the case," said the Angel.

51

"Of course," said the Vicar. "It is a great pity that was not the case. But at any rate you will oblige me if you do not obtrude your angelic nature. You will oblige everyone, in fact. There is a settled opinion that angels do not do this kind of thing. And nothing is more painful – as I can testify – than a decaying settled opinion... Settled opinions are mental teeth in more ways than one. For my own part," – the Vicar's hand passed over his eyes fox a moment – "I cannot but believe you are an angel... Surely I can believe my own eyes."

"We always do ours," said the Angel.

"And so do we, within limits."

Then the clock upon the mantel chimed seven, and almost simultaneously Mrs Hinijer announced dinner.

CHAPTER NINE

After Dinner

The Angel and the Vicar sat at dinner. The Vicar, with his napkin tucked in at his neck, watched the Angel struggling with his soup. "You will soon get into the way of it," said the Vicar. The knife and fork business was done awkwardly but with effect. The Angel looked furtively at Delia, the little waiting maid. When presently they sat cracking nuts – which the Angel found congenial enough – and the girl had gone, the Angel asked: "Was that a lady, too?"

"Well," said the Vicar (*crack*). "No – she is not a lady. She is a servant."

"Yes," said the Angel; "she *had* rather a nicer shape."

"You mustn't tell Mrs Mendham that," said the Vicar, covertly satisfied.

"She didn't stick out so much at the shoulders and hips, and there was more of her in between. And the colour of her robes was not discordant – simply neutral. And her face – "

"Mrs Mendham and her daughters had been playing tennis," said the Vicar, feeling he ought not to listen to detraction even of his mortal enemy. "Do you like these things – these nuts?"

"Very much," said the Angel. *Crack.*

53

"You see," said the Vicar (*Chum, chum, chum*). "For my own part I entirely believe you are an angel."

"Yes!" said the Angel.

"I shot you – I saw you flutter. It's beyond dispute. In my own mind. I admit it's curious and against my preconceptions, but – practically – I'm assured, perfectly assured in fact, that I saw what I certainly did see. But after the behaviour of these people. (*Crack*). I really don't see how we are to persuade people. Nowadays people are so very particular about evidence. So that I think there is a great deal to be said for the attitude you assume. Temporarily at least I think it would be best of you to do as you propose to do, and behave as a man as far as possible. Of course there is no knowing how or when you may go back. After what has happened (*Gluck, gluck, gluck* – as the Vicar refills his glass) – after what has happened I should not be surprised to see the side of the room fall away, and the hosts of heaven appear to take you away again – take us both away even. You have so far enlarged my imagination. All these years I have been forgetting Wonderland. But still – . It will certainly be wiser to break the thing gently to them."

"This life of yours," said the Angel. "I'm still in the dark about it. How do you begin?"

"Dear me!" said the Vicar. "Fancy having to explain that! We begin existence here, you know, as babies, silly pink helpless things wrapped in white, with goggling eyes, that yelp dismally at the Font. Then these babies grow larger and become even beautiful – when their faces are washed. And they continue to grow to a certain size. They become children, boys and girls, youths and maidens (*Crack*), young men and young women. That is the finest time in life, according to many – certainly the most beautiful. Full of great hopes and dreams, vague emotions and unexpected dangers."

"*That* was a maiden?" said the Angel, indicating the door through which Delia had disappeared.

"Yes," said the Vicar, "that was a maiden." And paused thoughtfully.

"And then?"

"Then," said the Vicar, "the glamour fades and life begins in earnest. The young men and young women pair off – most of them. They come to me shy and bashful, in smart ugly dresses, and I marry them. And then little pink babies come to them, and some of the youths and maidens that were, grow fat and vulgar, and some grow thin and shrewish, and their pretty complexions go, and they get a queer delusion of superiority over the younger people, and all the delight and glory goes out of their lives. So they call the delight and glory of the younger ones, Illusion. And then they begin to drop to pieces."

"Drop to pieces!" said the Angel. "How grotesque!"

"Their hair comes off and gets dull coloured or ashen grey," said the Vicar. "*I*, for instance." He bowed his head forward to show a circular shining patch the size of a florin. "And their teeth come out. Their faces collapse and become as wrinkled and dry as a shrivelled apple. 'Corrugated' you called mine. They care more and more for what they have to eat and to drink, and less and less for any of the other delights of life. Their limbs get loose in the joints, and their hearts slack, or little pieces from their lungs come coughing up. Pain…"

"Ah!" said the Angel.

"Pain comes into their lives more and more. And then they go. They do not like to go, but they have to – out of this world, very reluctantly, clutching its pain at last in their eagerness to stop…"

"Where do they go?"

"Once I thought I knew. But now I am older I know I do not know. We have a Legend – perhaps it is not a legend. One may be a churchman and disbelieve. Stokes says there is nothing in it…" The Vicar shook his head at the bananas.

"And you?" said the Angel. "Were you a little pink baby?"

"A little while ago I was a little pink baby."

"Were you robed then as you are now?"

"Oh no! Dear me! What a queer idea! Had long white clothes, I suppose, like the rest of them."

"And then you were a little boy?"

"A little boy."

"And then a glorious youth?"

"I was not a very glorious youth, I am afraid. I was sickly, and too poor to be radiant, and with a timid heart. I studied hard and pored over the dying thoughts of men long dead. So I lost the glory, and no maiden came to me, and the dulness of life began too soon."

"And you have your little pink babies?"

"None," said the Vicar with a scarce perceptible pause. "Yet all the same, as you see, I am beginning to drop to pieces. Presently my back will droop like a wilting flowerstalk. And then, in a few thousand days more I shall be done with, and I shall go out of this world of mine… Whither I do not know."

"And you have to eat like this every day?"

"Eat, and get clothes and keep this roof above me. There are some very disagreeable things in this world called Cold and Rain.

And the other people here – how and why is too long a story – have made me a kind of chorus to their lives. They bring their little pink babies to me and I have to say a name and some other things over each new pink baby. And when the children have grown to be youths and maidens, they come again and are confirmed. You will understand that better later. Then before they may join in couples and have pink babies of their own, they must come again and hear me read out of a book. They would be outcast, and no other maiden would speak to the maiden who had a little pink baby without I had read over her for twenty minutes out of my book. It's a necessary thing, as you will see. Odd as it may seem to you. And afterwards when they are falling to pieces, I try and persuade them of a strange world in which I scarcely believe myself, where life is altogether different from what they have had – or desire. And in the end, I bury them, and read out of my book to those who will presently follow into the unknown land. I stand at the beginning, and at the zenith, and at the setting of their lives. And on every seventh day, I who am a man myself, I who see no further than they do, talk to them of the Life to Come – the life of which we know nothing. If such a life there be. And slowly I drop to pieces amidst my prophesying."

"What a strange life!" said the Angel.

"Yes," said the Vicar. "What a strange life! But the thing that makes it strange to me is new. I had taken it as a matter of course until you came into my life.

"This life of ours is so insistent," said the Vicar. "It, and its petty needs, its temporary pleasures (*Crack*) swathe our souls about. While I am preaching to these people of mine of another life, some are ministering to one appetite and eating sweets, others – the old men – are slumbering, the youths glance at the

57

maidens, the grown men protrude white waistcoats and gold chains, pomp and vanity on a substratum of carnal substance, their wives flaunt garish bonnets at one another. And I go on droning away of the things unseen and unrealised – 'Eye hath not seen,' I read, 'nor ear heard, nor hath it entered into the imagination of man to conceive,' and I look up to catch an adult male immortal admiring the fit of a pair of three and sixpenny gloves. It is damping year after year. When I was ailing in my youth I felt almost the assurance of vision that beneath this temporary phantasm world was the real world – the enduring world of the Life Everlasting. But now – "

He glanced at his chubby white hand, fingering the stem of his glass. "I have put on flesh since then," he said. [*Pause.*]

"I have changed and developed very much. The battle of the Flesh and Spirit does not trouble me as it did. Every day I feel less confidence in my beliefs, and more in God. I live, I am afraid, a quiescent life, duties fairly done, a little ornithology and a little chess, a trifle of mathematical trifling. My times are in His hands – "

The Vicar sighed and became pensive. The Angel watched him, and the Angel's eyes were troubled with the puzzle of him. "Gluck, gluck, gluck," went the decanter as the Vicar refilled his glass.

2

So the Angel dined and talked to the Vicar, and presently the night came and he was overtaken by yawning.

"Yah—oh!" said the Angel suddenly. "Dear me! A higher power seemed suddenly to stretch my mouth open and a great breath of air went rushing down my throat."

"You yawned," said the Vicar. "Do you never yawn in the angelic country?"

"Never," said the Angel.

"And yet you are immortal! — I suppose you want to go to bed."

"Bed!" said the Angel. "Where's that?"

So the Vicar explained darkness to him and the art of going to bed. (The Angels, it seems, sleep only in order to dream, and dream, like primitive man, with their foreheads on their knees. And they sleep among the white poppy meadows in the heat of the day.) The Angel found the bedroom arrangements quaint enough.

"Why is everything raised up on big wooden legs?" he said. "You have the floor, and then you put everything you have upon a wooden quadruped. Why do you do it?" The Vicar explained with philosophical vagueness. The Angel burnt his finger in the candle-flame — and displayed an absolute ignorance of the elementary principles of combustion. He was merely charmed when a line of fire ran up the curtains. The Vicar had to deliver a lecture on fire so soon as the flame was extinguished. He had all kinds of explanations to make — even the soap needed explaining. It was an hour or more before the Angel was safely tucked in for the night.

"He's very beautiful," said the Vicar, descending the staircase, quite tired out; "and he's a real angel no doubt. But I am afraid he will be a dreadful anxiety, all the same, before he gets into our earthly way with things."

He seemed quite worried. He helped himself to an extra glass of sherry before he put away the wine in the cellaret.

3

The Curate stood in front of the looking-glass and solemnly divested himself of his collar.

"I never heard a more fantastic story," said Mrs Mendham from the basket chair. "The man must be mad. Are you sure – "

"Perfectly, my dear. I've told you every word, every incident – "

"*Well!*" said Mrs Mendham, and spread her hands. "There's no sense in it."

"Precisely, my dear."

"The Vicar," said Mrs Mendham, "must be mad."

"This hunchback is certainly one of the strangest creatures I've seen for a long time. Foreign looking, with a big bright coloured face and long brown hair... It can't have been cut for months!" The Curate put his studs carefully upon the shelf of the dressing-table. "And a kind of staring look about his eyes, and a simpering smile. Quite a silly looking person. Effeminate."

"But who *can* he be?" said Mrs Mendham.

"I can't imagine, my dear. Nor where he came from. He might be a chorister or something of that sort."

"But *why* should he be about the shrubbery...in that dreadful costume?"

"I don't know. The Vicar gave me no explanation. He simply said, 'Mendham, this is an Angel.'"

"I wonder if he drinks... They may have been bathing near the spring, of course," reflected Mrs Mendham. "But I noticed no other clothes on his arm."

The Curate sat down on his bed and unlaced his boots.

"It's a perfect mystery to me, my dear." (Flick, flick of laces.) "Hallucination is the only charitable – "

"You are sure, George, that it was *not* a woman."

"Perfectly," said the Curate.

"I know what men are, of course."

"It was a young man of nineteen or twenty," said the Curate.

"I can't understand it," said Mrs Mendham. "You say the creature is staying at the Vicarage?"

"Hilyer is simply mad," said the Curate. He got up and went padding round the room to the door to put out his boots. "To judge by his manner you would really think he believed this cripple was an Angel." ("Are your shoes out, dear?")

("They're just by the wardrobe"), said Mrs Mendham. "He always was a little queer, you know. There was always something childish about him... An Angel!"

The Curate came and stood by the fire, fumbling with his braces. Mrs Mendham liked a fire even in the summer. "He shirks all the serious problems in life and is always trifling with some new foolishness," said the Curate. "Angel indeed!" He laughed suddenly. "Hilyer *must* be mad," he said.

Mrs Mendham laughed too. "Even that doesn't explain the hunchback," she said.

"The hunchback must be mad too," said the Curate.

"It's the only way of explaining it in a sensible way," said Mrs Mendham. [*Pause.*]

"Angel or no angel," said Mrs Mendham, "I know what is due to me. Even supposing the man thought he *was* in the company of an angel, that is no reason why he should not behave like a gentleman."

"That is perfectly true."

"You will write to the Bishop, of course?"

Mendham coughed. "No, I shan't write to the Bishop," said Mendham. "I think it seems a little disloyal... And he took no notice of the last, you know."

"But surely – "

"I shall write to Austin. In confidence. He will be sure to tell the Bishop, you know. And you must remember, my dear – "

"That Hilyer can dismiss you, you were going to say. My dear, the man's much too weak! *I* should have a word to say about that. And besides, you do all his work for him. Practically, we manage the parish from end to end. I do not know what would become of the poor if it was not for me. They'd have free quarters in the Vicarage tomorrow. There is that Goody Ansell – "

"I know, my dear," said the Curate, turning away and proceeding with his undressing. "You were telling me about her only this afternoon."

4

And thus in the little bedroom over the gable we reach a first resting place in this story. And as we have been hard at it, getting our story spread out before you, it may be perhaps well to recapitulate a little.

Looking back you will see that much has been done; we began with a blaze of light "not uniform but broken all over by curving flashes like the waving of swords," and the sound of a mighty harping, and the advent of an Angel with polychromatic wings.

Swiftly, dexterously, as the reader must admit, wings have been clipped, halo handled off, the glory clapped into coat and

62

trousers, and the Angel made for all practical purposes a man, under a suspicion of being either a lunatic or an impostor. You have heard too, or at least been able to judge, what the Vicar and the Doctor and the Curate's wife thought of the strange arrival. And further remarkable opinions are to follow.

The afterglow of the summer sunset in the north-west darkens into night and the Angel sleeps, dreaming himself back in the wonderful world where it is always light, and everyone is happy, where fire does not burn and ice does not chill; where rivulets of starlight go streaming through the amaranthine meadows, out to the seas of Peace. He dreams, and it seems to him that once more his wings glow with a thousand colours and flash through the crystal air of the world from which he has come.

So he dreams. But the Vicar lies awake, too perplexed for dreaming. Chiefly he is troubled by the possibilities of Mrs Mendham; but the evening's talk has opened strange vistas in his mind, and he is stimulated by a sense as of something seen darkly by the indistinct vision of a hitherto unsuspected wonderland lying about his world. For twenty years now he has held his village living and lived his daily life, protected by his familiar creed, by the clamour of the details of life, from any mystical dreaming. But now interweaving with the familiar bother of his persecuting neighbour, is an altogether unfamiliar sense of strange new things.

There was something ominous in the feeling. Once, indeed, it rose above all other considerations, and in a kind of terror he blundered out of bed, bruised his shins very convincingly, found the matches at last, and lit a candle to assure himself of the reality of his own customary world again. But on the whole the more tangible trouble was the Mendham avalanche. Her tongue seemed to be hanging above him like the sword of Damocles. What might she not say of this business, before her indignant imagination came to rest?

And while the successful captor of the Strange Bird was sleeping thus uneasily, Gully of Sidderton was carefully unloading his gun after a wearisome blank day, and Sandy Bright was on his knees in prayer, with the window carefully fastened. Annie Durgan was sleeping hard with her mouth open, and Amory's mother was dreaming of washing, and both of them had long since exhausted the topics of the Sound and the Glare. Lumpy Durgan was sitting up in his bed, now crooning the fragment of a tune and now listening intently for a sound he had heard once and longed to hear again. As for the solicitor's clerk at Iping Hanger, he was trying to write poetry about a confectioner's girl at Portburdock, and the Strange Bird was quite out of his head. But the ploughman who had seen it on the confines of Siddermorton Park had a black eye. That had been one of the more tangible consequences of a little argument about birds' legs in the "Ship." It is worthy of this passing mention, since it is probably the only known instance of an Angel causing anything of the kind.

Chapter Ten

Morning

The Vicar going to call the Angel, found him dressed and leaning out of his window. It was a glorious morning, still dewy, and the rising sunlight slanting round the corner of the house, struck warm and yellow upon the hillside. The birds were astir in the hedges and shrubbery. Up the hillside – for it was late in August – a plough drove slowly. The Angel's chin rested upon his hands and he did not turn as the Vicar came up to him.

"How's the wing?" said the Vicar.

"I'd forgotten it," said the Angel. "Is that yonder a man?"

The Vicar looked. "That's a ploughman."

"Why does he go to and fro like that? Does it amuse him?"

"He's ploughing. That's his work."

"Work! Why does he do it? It seems a monotonous thing to do."

"It is," admitted the Vicar. "But he has to do it to get a living, you know. To get food to eat and all that kind of thing."

"How curious!" said the Angel. "Do all men have to do that? Do you?"

"Oh, no. He does it for me; does my share."

"Why?" asked the Angel.

"Oh! in return for things I do for him, you know. We go in for division of labour in this world. Exchange is no robbery."

"I see," said the Angel, with his eyes still on the ploughman's heavy movements.

"What do you do for him?"

"That seems an easy question to you," said the Vicar, "but really! – it's difficult. Our social arrangements are rather complicated. It's impossible to explain these things all at once, before breakfast. Don't you feel hungry?"

"I think I do," said the Angel slowly, still at the window; and then abruptly, "Somehow I can't help thinking that ploughing must be far from enjoyable."

"Possibly," said the Vicar, "very possibly. But breakfast is ready. Won't you come down?"

The Angel left the window reluctantly.

"Our society," explained the Vicar on the staircase, "is a complicated organisation."

"Yes?"

"And it is so arranged that some do one thing and some another."

"And that lean, bent old man trudges after that heavy blade of iron pulled by a couple of horses while we go down to eat?"

"Yes. You will find it is perfectly just. Ah! mushrooms and poached eggs! It's the Social System. Pray be seated. Possibly it strikes you as unfair?"

"I'm puzzled," said the Angel.

"The drink I'm sending you is called coffee," said the Vicar. "I daresay you are. When I was a young man I was puzzled in the same way. But afterwards comes a Broader View of Things. (These black things are called mushrooms; they look beautiful.)

Other Considerations. All men are brothers, of course, but some are younger brothers, so to speak. There is work that requires culture and refinement, and work in which culture and refinement would be an impediment. And the rights of property must not be forgotten. One must render unto Cæsar... Do you know, instead of explaining this matter now (this is yours), I think I will lend you a little book to read (*chum, chum, chum* – these mushrooms are well up to their appearance), which sets the whole thing out very clearly."

CHAPTER ELEVEN

The Violin

After breakfast the Vicar went into the little room next his study to find a book on Political Economy for the Angel to read. For the Angel's social ignorances were clearly beyond any verbal explanations. The door stood ajar.

"What is that?" said the Angel, following him. "A violin!" He took it down.

"You play?" said the Vicar.

The Angel had the bow in his hand, and by way of answer drove it across the strings. The quality of the note made the Vicar turn suddenly.

The Angel's hand tightened on the instrument. The bow flew back and flickered, and an air the Vicar had never heard before danced in his ears. The Angel shifted the fiddle under his dainty chin and went on playing, and as he played his eyes grew bright and his lips smiled. At first he looked at the Vicar, then his expression became abstracted. He seemed no longer to look at the Vicar, but through him, at something beyond, something in his memory or his imagination, something infinitely remote, undreamt of hitherto...

The Vicar tried to follow the music. The air reminded him of a flame, it rushed up, shone, flickered and danced, passed and reappeared. No! – it did not reappear! Another air – like it and unlike it, shot up after it, wavered, vanished. Then another, the same and not the same. It reminded him of the flaring tongues that palpitate and change above a newly lit fire. There are two airs – or *motifs*, which is it? – thought the Vicar. He knew remarkably little of musical technique. They go dancing up, one pursuing the other, out of the fire of the incantation, pursuing, fluctuating, turning, up into the sky. There below was the fire burning, a flame without fuel upon a level space, and there two flirting butterflies of sound, dancing away from it, up, one over another, swift, abrupt, uncertain.

"Flirting butterflies were they!" What was the Vicar thinking of? Where was he? In the little room next to his study, of course! And the Angel standing in front of him smiling into his face, playing the violin, and looking through him as though he was only a window – . That *motif* again, a yellow flare, spread fanlike by a gust, and now one, then with a swift eddying upward flight the other, the two things of fire and light pursuing one another again up into that clear immensity.

The study and the realities of life suddenly faded out of the Vicar's eyes, grew thinner and thinner like a mist that dissolves into air, and he and the Angel stood together on a pinnacle of wrought music, about which glittering melodies circled, and vanished, and reappeared. He was in the land of Beauty, and once more the glory of heaven was upon the Angel's face, and the glowing delights of colour pulsated in his wings. Himself the Vicar could not see. But I cannot tell you of the vision of that great and spacious land, of its incredible openness, and height, and nobility. For there is no space there like ours, no time as we know it; one must needs speak by bungling metaphors and own in bitterness after all that one has failed. And it was only a vision. The wonderful creatures flying through the aether saw them not as they stood there, flew through them as one might pass through a whisp of mist. The Vicar lost all sense of duration, all sense of necessity –

"Ah!" said the Angel, suddenly putting down the fiddle.

The Vicar had forgotten the book on Political Economy, had forgotten everything until the Angel had done. For a minute he sat quite still. Then he woke up with a start. He was sitting on the old iron-bound chest.

"Really," he said slowly, "you are very clever."

He looked about him in a puzzled way. "I had a kind of vision while you were playing. I seemed to see – . What did I see? It has gone."

He stood up with a dazzled expression upon his face. "I shall never play the violin again," he said. "I wish you would take it to your room – and keep it – . And play to me again. I did not know anything of music until I heard you play. I do not feel as though I had ever heard any music before."

He stared at the Angel, then about him at the room. "I have never felt anything of this kind with music before," he said. He shook his head. "I shall never play again."

CHAPTER TWELVE

The Angel Explores the Village

Very unwisely, as I think, the Vicar allowed the Angel to go down into the village by himself, to enlarge his ideas of humanity. Unwisely, because how was he to imagine the reception the Angel would receive? Not thoughtlessly, I am afraid. He had always carried himself with decorum in the village, and the idea of a slow procession through the little street with all the inevitable curious remarks, explanations, pointings, was too much for him. The Angel might do the strangest things, the village was certain to think them. Peering faces. "Who's he got now?" Besides, was it not his duty to prepare his sermon in good time? The Angel, duly directed, went down cheerfully by himself – still innocent of most of the peculiarities of the human as distinguished from the angelic turn of mind.

The Angel walked slowly, his white hands folded behind his hunched back, his sweet face looking this way and that. He peered curiously into the eyes of the people he met. A little child picking a bunch of vetch and honeysuckle looked in his face, and forthwith came and put them in his hand. It was about the only kindness he had from a human being (saving only the Vicar and one other). He heard Mother Gustick scolding that granddaughter of hers as he passed the door. "You *Brazen* Faggit – you!" said Mother Gustick. "You Trumpery Baggage!"

The Angel stopped, startled at the strange sounds of Mother Gustick's voice. "Put yer best clo'es on, and yer feather in yer 'at, and off you goes to meet 'en, fal lal, and me at 'ome slaving for ye. 'Tis a Fancy Lady you'll be wantin' to be, my gal, a walkin' Touch and Go, with yer idleness and finery – "

The voice ceased abruptly, and a great peace came upon the battered air. "Most grotesque and strange!" said the Angel, still surveying this wonderful box of discords. "Walking Touch and Go!" He did not know that Mrs Gustick had suddenly become aware of his existence, and was scrutinising his appearance through the window-blind. Abruptly the door flew open, and she stared out into the Angel's face. A strange apparition, grey and dusty hair, and the dirty pink dress unhooked to show the stringy throat, a discoloured gargoyle, presently to begin spouting incomprehensible abuse.

"Now, then, Mister," began Mrs Gustick. "Have ye nothin' better to do than listen at people's doors for what you can pick up?"

The Angel stared at her in astonishment.

"D'year!" said Mrs Gustick, evidently very angry indeed. "Listenin'."

"Have you any objection to my hearing…"

"Object to my hearing! Course I have! Whad yer think? You aint such a Ninny…"

"But if ye didn't want me to hear, why did you cry out so loud? I thought…"

"*You thought!* Softie – that's what *you* are! You silly girt staring Gaby, what don't know any better than to come holding yer girt mouth wide open for all that you can catch holt on? And then off up there to tell! You great Fat-Faced, Tale-Bearin' Silly-Billy! I'd be ashamed to come poking and peering round quiet people's houses..."

The Angel was surprised to find that some inexplicable quality in her voice excited the most disagreeable sensations in him and a strong desire to withdraw. But, resisting this, he stood listening politely (as the custom is in the Angelic Land, so long as anyone is speaking). The entire eruption was beyond his comprehension. He could not perceive any reason for the sudden projection of this vituperative head, out of infinity, so to speak. And questions without a break for an answer were outside his experience altogether.

Mrs Gustick proceeded with her characteristic fluency, assured him he was no gentleman, enquired if he called himself one, remarked that every tramp did as much nowadays, compared him to a Stuck Pig, marvelled at his impudence, asked him if he wasn't ashamed of himself standing there, enquired if he was rooted to the ground, was curious to be told what he meant by it, wanted to know whether he robbed a scarecrow for his clothes, suggested that an abnormal vanity prompted his behaviour, enquired if his mother knew he was out, and finally remarking, "I got somethin'll move you, my gentleman," disappeared with a ferocious slamming of the door.

The interval struck the Angel as singularly peaceful. His whirling mind had time to analyse his sensations. He ceased bowing and smiling, and stood merely astonished.

"This is a curious painful feeling," said the Angel. "Almost worse than Hungry, and quite different. When one is hungry one

75

wants to eat. I suppose she was a woman. Here one wants to get away. I suppose I might just as well go."

He turned slowly and went down the road meditating. He heard the cottage door re-open, and turning his head, saw through intervening scarlet runners Mrs Gustick with a steaming saucepan full of boiling cabbage water in her hand.

" 'Tis well you went, Mister Stolen Breeches," came the voice of Mrs Gustick floating down through the vermilion blossoms. "Don't you come peeping and prying round this yer cottage again or I'll learn ye manners, I will!"

The Angel stood in a state of considerable perplexity. He had no desire to come within earshot of the cottage again – ever. He did not understand the precise import of the black pot, but his general impression was entirely disagreeable. There was no explaining it.

"I *mean* it!" said Mrs Gustick, crescendo. "Drat it! – I *mean* it."

The Angel turned and went on, a dazzled look in his eyes.

"She was very grotesque!" said the Angel. "*Very*. Much more than the little man in black. And she means it. – But what she means I don't know!..." He became silent. "I suppose they all mean something," he said, presently, still perplexed.

2

Then the Angel came in sight of the forge, where Sandy Bright's brother was shoeing a horse for the carter from Upmorton. Two hobbledehoys were standing by the forge staring in a bovine way at the proceedings. As the Angel approached these two and then the carter turned slowly through an angle of thirty degrees and watched his approach, staring quietly and steadily at him. The expression on their faces was one of abstract interest.

The Angel became self-conscious for the first time in his life. He drew nearer, trying to maintain an amiable expression on his face, an expression that beat in vain against their granitic stare. His hands were behind him. He smiled pleasantly, looking curiously at the (to him) incomprehensible employment of the smith. But the battery of eyes seemed to angle for his regard. Trying to meet the three pairs at once, the Angel lost his alertness and stumbled over a stone. One of the yokels gave a sarcastic cough, and was immediately covered with confusion at the Angel's enquiring gaze, nudging his companion with his elbow to cover his disorder. None spoke, and the Angel did not speak.

So soon as the Angel had passed, one of the three hummed this tune in an aggressive tone.

Then all three of them laughed. One tried to sing something and found his throat contained phlegm. The Angel proceeded on his way.

"Who's *e* then?" said the second hobbledehoy.

"Ping, ping, ping," went the blacksmith's hammer.

"Spose he's one of these here foweners," said the carter from Upmorton. "Däamned silly fool he do look to be sure."

"'Tas the way with them foweners," said the first hobbledehoy sagely.

"Got something very like the 'ump," said the carter from Upmorton. "Dää-ä-ämned if 'E ent."

Then the silence healed again, and they resumed their quiet expressionless consideration of the Angel's retreating figure.

"Very like the 'ump et is," said the carter after an enormous pause.

3

The Angel went on through the village, finding it all wonderful enough. "They begin, and just a little while and then they end," he said to himself in a puzzled voice. "But what are they doing meanwhile?" Once he heard some invisible mouth chant inaudible words to the tune the man at the forge had hummed.

"That's the poor creature the Vicar shot with that great gun of his," said Sarah Glue (of 1, Church Cottages) peering over the blind.

"He looks Frenchified," said Susan Hopper, peering through the interstices of that convenient veil on curiosity.

"He has sweet eyes," said Sarah Glue, who had met them for a moment.

The Angel sauntered on. The postman passed him and touched his hat to him; further down was a dog asleep in the sun. He went on and saw Mendham, who nodded distantly and hurried past. (The Curate did not care to be seen talking to an angel in the village, until more was known about him.) There came from one of the houses the sound of a child screaming in a passion, that brought a puzzled look to the angelic face. Then the Angel reached the bridge below the last of the houses, and stood leaning over the parapet watching the glittering little cascade from the mill.

"They begin, and just a little while, and then they end," said the weir from the mill. The water raced under the bridge, green and dark, and streaked with foam.

Beyond the mill rose the square tower of the church, with the churchyard behind it, a spray of tombstones and wooden headboards splashed up the hillside. A half dozen of beech trees framed the picture.

Then the Angel heard a shuffling of feet and the grind of wheels behind him, and turning his head saw a man dressed in dirty brown rags and a felt hat grey with dust, who was standing with a slight swaying motion and fixedly regarding the Angelic back. Beyond him was another almost equally dirty, pushing a knife grinder's barrow over the bridge.

"Mornin'," said the first person smiling weakly. "Goomorn'." He arrested an escaping hiccough.

The Angel stared at him. He had never seen a really fatuous smile before. "Who are you?" said the Angel.

The fatuous smile faded. "No your business whoaaam. Wishergoomorn."

"Carm on," said the man with the grindstone, passing on his way.

"Wishergoomorn," said the dirty man, in a tone of extreme aggravation. "Carncher Answerme?"

"Carm *on* you fool!" said the man with the grindstone – receding.

"I don't understand," said the Angel.

"Donunderstan'. Sim'l enough. Wishergoomorn'. Willyanswerme? Wontchr? gemwishergem goomorn. Cusom answer goomorn. No gem. Haverteachyer."

79

The Angel was puzzled. The drunken man stood swaying for a moment, then he made an unsteady snatch at his hat and threw it down at the Angel's feet. "Ver well," he said, as one who decides great issues.

"*Carm* on!" said the voice of the man with the grindstone – stopping perhaps twenty yards off.

"You *wan* fight, you – " the Angel failed to catch the word. "I'll show yer, not answer gem's goomorn."

He began to struggle with his jacket. "Think I'm drun," he said, "I show yer." The man with the grindstone sat down on the shaft to watch. "Carm on," he said. The jacket was intricate, and the drunken man began to struggle about the road, in his attempts to extricate himself, breathing threatenings and slaughter. Slowly the Angel began to suspect, remotely enough, that these demonstrations were hostile. "Mur wun know yer when I done wi' yer," said the drunken man, coat almost over his head.

At last the garment lay on the ground, and through the frequent interstices of his reminiscences of a waistcoat, the drunken tinker displayed a fine hairy and muscular body to the Angel's observant eyes. He squared up in masterly fashion.

"Take the paint off yer," he remarked, advancing and receding, fists up and elbows out.

"Carm on," floated down the road.

The Angel's attention was concentrated on two huge hairy black fists, that swayed and advanced and retreated. "Come on d'yer say? I'll show yer," said the gentleman in rags, and then with extraordinary ferocity; "My crikey! I'll show yer."

Suddenly he lurched forward, and with a newborn instinct and raising a defensive arm as he did so, the Angel stepped aside to avoid him. The fist missed the Angelic shoulder by a hairsbreadth, and the tinker collapsed in a heap with his face against the parapet of the bridge. The Angel hesitated over the writhing dusty heap of blasphemy for a moment, and then turned towards the man's companion up the road. "Lemmeget up," said the man on the bridge. "Lemmeget up, you swine. I'll show yer."

A strange disgust, a quivering repulsion came upon the Angel. He walked slowly away from the drunkard towards the man with the grindstone.

"What does it all mean?" said the Angel. "I don't understand it."

"Dam fool!...say's it's 'is silver weddin'," answered the man with the grindstone, evidently much annoyed; and then, in a tone of growing impatience, he called down the road once more; "Carm on!"

"Silver wedding!" said the Angel. "What is a silver wedding?"

"Jest is rot," said the man on the barrow. "But 'E's always 'avin' some 'scuse like that. Fair sickenin' it is. Lars week it wus 'is bloomin' birthday, and *then* 'e ad'nt 'ardly got sober orf a comlimentary drunk to my noo barrer. (*Carm* on, you fool.)"

"But I don't understand," said the Angel. "Why does he sway about so? Why does he keep on trying to pick up his hat like that – and missing it?"

"*Why!*" said the tinker. "Well this *is* a blasted innocent country! *Why!* Because 'E's blind! Wot else? (Carm on – *Dam* yer.) Because 'E's just as full as 'E can 'old. That's *why!*"

The Angel noticing the tone of the second tinker's voice, judged it wiser not to question him further. But he stood by the

81

grindstone and continued to watch the mysterious evolutions on the bridge.

"Carm on! I shall 'ave to go and pick up that 'at I suppose… 'E's always at it. I ne'er 'ad such a blooming pard before. *Always* at it, 'e is."

The man with the barrow meditated. "Taint as if 'e was a gentleman and 'adnt no livin' to get. An' 'e's such a reckless fool when 'e gets a bit on. Goes offerin' out everyone 'e meets. (There you go!) I'm blessed if 'e didn't offer out a 'ole bloomin' Salvation Army. No judgment in it. (Oh! *Carm* on! *Carm* on!) 'Ave to go and pick this bloomin' 'at up now I s'pose. 'E don't care, *wot* trouble 'e gives."

The Angel watched the second tinker walk back, and, with affectionate blasphemy, assist the first to his hat and his coat. Then he turned, absolutely mystified, towards the village again.

4

After that incident the Angel walked along past the mill and round behind the church, to examine the tombstones.

"This seems to be the place where they put the broken pieces," said the Angel – reading the inscriptions. "Curious word – relict! Resurgam! Then they are not done with quite. What a huge pile it requires to keep her down… It is spirited of her."

"Hawkins?" said the Angel softly… "*Hawkins?* The name is strange to me… He did not die then… It is plain enough – Joined the Angelic Hosts, May 17, 1863. He must have felt as much out of place as I do down here. But I wonder why they put that little pot thing on the top of this monument. Curious! There are several others about – little stone pots with a rag of stiff stone drapery over them."

Just then the boys came pouring out of the National School, and first one and then several stopped agape at the Angel's crooked black figure among the white tombs. "Ent 'e gart a bääk on en!" remarked one critic.

" 'E's got 'air like a girl!" said another.

The Angel turned towards them. He was struck by the queer little heads sticking up over the lichenous wall. He smiled faintly at their staring faces, and then turned to marvel at the iron railings that enclosed the Fitz-Jarvis tomb. "A queer air of uncertainty," he said. "Slabs, piles of stone, these railings... Are they afraid?... Do these Dead ever try and get up again? There's an air of repression – fortification – "

"Gét yer 'air cut, Gét yer 'air cut," sang three little boys together.

"Curious these Human Beings are!" said the Angel. "That man yesterday wanted to cut off my wings, now these little creatures want me to cut off my hair! And the man on the bridge offered to take the 'paint' off me. They will leave nothing of me soon."

"Where did you get that 'at?" sang another little boy. "Where did you get them clo'es?"

"They ask questions that they evidently do not want answered," said the Angel. "I can tell from the tone." He looked thoughtfully at the little boys. "I don't understand the methods of Human intercourse. These are probably friendly advances, a kind of ritual. But I don't know the responses. I think I will go back to the little fat man in black, with the gold chain across his stomach, and ask him to explain. It is difficult."

He turned towards the lych gate. "*Oh!*" said one of the little boys, in a shrill falsetto, and threw a beech-nut husk. It came bounding across the churchyard path. The Angel stopped in surprise.

This made all the little boys laugh. A second imitating the first, said "*Oh!*" and hit the Angel. His astonishment was really delicious. They all began crying "*Oh!*" and throwing beech-nut husks. One hit the Angel's hand, another stung him smartly by the ear. The Angel made ungainly movements towards them. He spluttered some expostulation and made for the roadway. The little boys were amazed and shocked at his discomfiture and cowardice. Such sawney behaviour could not be encouraged. The pelting grew vigorously. You may perhaps be able to imagine those vivid moments, daring small boys running in close and delivering shots, milder small boys rushing round behind with flying discharges. Milton Screever's mongrel dog was roused to yelping ecstacy at the sight, and danced (full of wild imaginings) nearer and nearer to the angelic legs.

"Hi, hi!" said a vigorous voice. "I never did! Where's Mr Jarvis? Manners, manners! you young rascals."

The youngsters scattered right and left, some over the wall into the playground, some down the street.

"Frightful pest these boys are getting!" said Crump, coming up. "I'm sorry they have been annoying you."

The Angel seemed quite upset. "I don't understand," he said. "These Human ways…"

"Yes, of course. Unusual to you. How's your excrescence?"

"My what?" said the Angel.

"Bifid limb, you know. How is it? Now, you're down this way, come in. Come in and let me have a look at it again. You young

84

roughs! And meanwhile these little louts of ours will be getting off home. They're all alike in these villages. *Can't* understand anything abnormal. See an odd-looking stranger. Chuck a stone. No imagination beyond the parish... (I'll give you physic if I catch you annoying strangers again.)... I suppose it's what one might expect... Come along this way."

So the Angel, horribly perplexed still, was hurried into the surgery to have his wound redressed.

CHAPTER THIRTEEN

Lady Hammergallow's View

In Siddermorton Park is Siddermorton House, where old Lady Hammergallow lives, chiefly upon Burgundy and the little scandals of the village, a dear old lady with a ropy neck, a ruddled countenance and spasmodic gusts of odd temper, whose three remedies for all human trouble among her dependents are, a bottle of gin, a pair of charity blankets, or a new crown piece. The House is a mile-and-a-half out of Siddermorton. Almost all the village is hers, saving a fringe to the south which belongs to Sir John Gotch, and she rules it with an autocratic rule, refreshing in these days of divided government. She orders and forbids marriages, drives objectionable people out of the village by the simple expedient of raising their rent, dismisses labourers, obliges heretics to go to church, and made Susan Dangett, who wanted to call her little girl 'Euphemia,' have the infant christened 'Mary-Anne.' She is a sturdy Broad Protestant and disapproves of the Vicar's going bald like a tonsure. She is on the Village Council, which obsequiously trudges up the hill and over the moor to her, and (as she is a trifle deaf) speaks all its speeches into her speaking trumpet instead of a rostrum. She takes no interest now in politics, but until last year she was an active enemy of "that Gladstone." She has parlour maids instead of footmen to do her waiting, because of Hockley, the American stockbroker, and his four Titans in plush.

She exercises what is almost a fascination upon the village. If in the bar-parlour of the Cat and Cornucopia you swear by God no one would be shocked, but if you swore by Lady Hammergallow they would probably be shocked enough to turn you out of the room. When she drives through Siddermorton she always calls upon Bessy Flump, the post-mistress, to hear all that has happened, and then upon Miss Finch, the dressmaker, to check back Bessy Flump. Sometimes she calls upon the Vicar, sometimes upon Mrs Mendham whom she snubs, and even sometimes on Crump. Her sparkling pair of greys almost ran over the Angel as he was walking down to the village.

"So *that's* the genius!" said Lady Hammergallow, and turned and looked at him through the gilt glasses on a stick that she always carried in her shrivelled and shaky hand. "Lunatic indeed! The poor creature has rather a pretty face. I'm sorry I've missed him."

But she went on to the vicarage nevertheless, and demanded news of it all. The conflicting accounts of Miss Flump, Miss Finch, Mrs Mendham, Crump, and Mrs Jehoram had puzzled her immensely. The Vicar, hard pressed, did all he could to say into her speaking trumpet what had really happened. He toned down the wings and the saffron robe. But he felt the case was hopeless. He spoke of his protégé as "Mr" Angel. He addressed pathetic asides to the kingfisher. The old lady noticed his confusion. Her queer old head went jerking backwards and forwards, now the speaking trumpet in his face when he had nothing to say, then the shrunken eyes peering at him, oblivious of the explanation that was coming from his lips. A great many Ohs! and Ahs! She caught some fragments certainly.

"You have asked him to stop with you – indefinitely?" said Lady Hammergallow with a Great Idea taking shape rapidly in her mind.

"I did – perhaps inadvertently – make such – "

"And you don't know where he comes from?"

"Not at all."

"Nor who his father is, I suppose?" said Lady Hammergallow mysteriously.

"No," said the Vicar.

"*Now!*" said Lady Hammergallow archly, and keeping her glasses to her eye, she suddenly dug at his ribs with her trumpet.

"My *dear* Lady Hammergallow!"

"I thought so. Don't think *I* would blame you, Mr Hilyer." She gave a corrupt laugh that she delighted in. "The world is the world, and men are men. And the poor boy's a cripple, eh? A kind of judgment. In mourning, I noticed. It reminds me of the *Scarlet Letter*. The mother's dead, I suppose. It's just as well. Really – I'm not a *narrow* woman – I *respect* you for having him. Really I do."

"But, *Lady* Hammergallow!"

"Don't spoil everything by denying it. It is so very, very plain, to a woman of the world. That Mrs Mendham! She amuses me with her suspicions. Such odd ideas! In a Curate's wife. But I hope it didn't happen when you were in orders."

"Lady Hammergallow, I protest. Upon my word."

"Mr Hilyer, I protest. I *know*. Not anything you can say will alter my opinion one jot. Don't try. I never suspected you were nearly such an interesting man."

"But this suspicion is unendurable!"

"We will help him together, Mr Hilyer. You may rely upon me. It is most romantic." She beamed benevolence.

"But, Lady Hammergallow, I *must* speak!"

She gripped her ear trumpet resolutely, and held it before her and shook her head.

"He has quite a genius for music, Vicar, so I hear?"

"I can assure you most solemnly – "

"I thought so. And being a cripple – "

"You are under a most cruel – "

"I thought that if his gift is really what that Jehoram woman says."

"An unjustifiable suspicion that ever a man – "

("I don't think much of her judgment, of course.")

"Consider my position. Have I gained *no* character?"

"It might be possible to do something for him as a performer."

"Have I – (*Bother! It's no good!*)"

"And so, dear Vicar, I propose to give him an opportunity of showing us what he can do. I have been thinking it all over as I drove here. On Tuesday next, I will invite just a few people of taste, and he shall bring his violin. Eigh? And if that goes well, I will see if I can get some introductions and really *push* him."

"But *Lady*, Lady Hammergallow."

"Not another word!" said Lady Hammergallow, still resolutely holding her speaking-trumpet before her and clutching her eyeglasses. "I really must not leave those horses. Cutler is so annoyed if I keep them too long. He finds waiting tedious, poor man, unless there is a public-house near." She made for the door.

"*Damn!*" said the Vicar, under his breath. He had never used the word since he had taken orders. It shows you how an Angel's visit may disorganise a man.

He stood under the verandah watching the carriage drive away. The world seemed coming to pieces about him. Had he lived a virtuous celibate life for thirty odd years in vain? The things of which these people thought him capable! He stood and stared at the green cornfield opposite, and down at the straggling village. It seemed real enough. And yet for the first time in his life there was a queer doubt of its reality. He rubbed his chin, then turned and went slowly upstairs to his dressing-room, and sat for a long time staring at a garment of some yellow texture. "Know his father!" he said. "And he is immortal, and was fluttering about his heaven when my ancestors were marsupials... I wish he was there now."

He got up and began to feel the robe.

"I wonder how they get such things," said the Vicar. Then he went and stared out of the window. "I suppose everything is wonderful, even the rising and setting of the sun. I suppose there is no adamantine ground for any belief. But one gets into a regular way of taking things. This disturbs it. I seem to be waking up to the Invisible. It is the strangest of uncertainties. I have not felt so stirred and unsettled since my adolescence."

CHAPTER FOURTEEN

Further Adventures of the Angel in the Village

"That's all right," said Crump when the bandaging was replaced. "It's a trick of memory, no doubt, but these excrescences of yours don't seem nearly so large as they did yesterday. I suppose they struck me rather forcibly. Stop and have lunch with me now you're down here. Midday meal, you know. The youngsters will be swallowed up by school again in the afternoon.

"I never saw anything heal so well in my life," he said, as they walked into the dining-room. "Your blood and flesh must be as clean and free from bacteria as they make 'em. Whatever stuff there is in your head," he added *sotto voce*.

At lunch he watched the Angel narrowly, and talked to draw him out.

"Journey tire you yesterday?" he said suddenly.

"Journey!" said the Angel. "Oh! my wings felt a little stiff."

("Not to be had,") said Crump to himself. ("Suppose I must enter into it.")

"So you flew all the way, eigh? No conveyance?"

"There wasn't any way," explained the Angel, taking mustard. "I was flying up a symphony with some Griffins and Fiery

93

Cherubim, and suddenly everything went dark and I was in this world of yours."

"Dear me!" said Crump. "And that's why you haven't any luggage." He drew his serviette across his mouth, and a smile flickered in his eyes.

"I suppose you know this world of ours pretty well? Watching us over the adamantine walls and all that kind of thing. Eigh?"

"Not very well. We dream of it sometimes. In the moonlight, when the Nightmares have fanned us to sleep with their wings."

"Ah, yes – of course," said Crump. "Very poetical way of putting it. Won't you take some Burgundy? It's just beside you."

"There's a persuasion in this world, you know, that Angels' Visits are by no means infrequent. Perhaps some of your – friends have travelled? They are supposed to come down to deserving persons in prisons, and do refined Nautches and that kind of thing. Faust business, you know."

"I've never heard of anything of the kind," said the Angel.

"Only the other day a lady whose baby was my patient for the time being – indigestion – assured me that certain facial contortions the little creature made indicated that it was Dreaming of Angels. In the novels of Mrs Henry Wood that is spoken of as an infallible symptom of an early departure. I suppose you can't throw any light on that obscure pathological manifestation?"

"I don't understand it at all," said the Angel, puzzled, and not clearly apprehending the Doctor's drift.

("Getting huffy,") said Crump to himself. ("Sees I'm poking fun at him.") "There's one thing I'm curious about. Do the new arrivals complain much about their medical attendants? I've always fancied there must be a good deal of hydropathic talk just at first. I was looking at that picture in the Academy only this June..."

"New Arrivals!" said the Angel. "I really don't follow you."

The Doctor stared. "Don't they come?"

"Come!" said the Angel. "Who?"

"The people who die here."

"After they've gone to pieces here?"

"That's the general belief, you know."

"People, like the woman who screamed out of the door, and the black-faced man and his volutations and the horrible little things that threw husks! – certainly not. *I* never saw such creatures before I fell into this world."

"Oh! but come!" said the Doctor. "You'll tell me next your official robes are not white and that you can't play the harp."

"There's no such thing as white in the Angelic Land," said the Angel. "It's that queer blank colour you get by mixing up all the others."

"Why, my dear Sir!" said the doctor, suddenly altering his tone, "you positively know nothing about the Land you come from. White's the very essence of it."

The Angel stared at him. Was the man jesting? He looked perfectly serious.

"Look here," said Crump, and getting up, he went to the sideboard on which a copy of the Parish Magazine was lying. He brought it round to the Angel and opened it at the coloured supplement. "Here's some *real* angels," he said. "You see it's not simply the wings make the Angel. White you see, with a curly whisp of robe, sailing up into the sky with their wings furled. Those are angels on the best authority. Hydroxyl kind of hair.

One has a bit of a harp, you see, and the other is helping this wingless lady – kind of larval Angel, you know – upward."

"Oh! but really!" said the Angel, "those are not angels at all."

"But they *are*," said Crump, putting the magazine back on the sideboard and resuming his seat with an air of intense satisfaction. "I can assure you I have the *best* authority..."

"I can assure you..."

Crump tucked in the corners of his mouth and shook his head from side to side even as he had done to the Vicar. "No good," he said, "can't alter our ideas just because an irresponsible visitor..."

"If these are angels," said the Angel, "then I have never been in the Angelic Land."

"Precisely," said Crump, ineffably self-satisfied; "that was just what I was getting at."

The Angel stared at him for a minute round-eyed, and then was seized for the second time by the human disorder of laughter.

"Ha, ha, ha!" said Crump, joining in. "I *thought* you were not quite so mad as you seemed. Ha, ha, ha!"

And for the rest of the lunch they were both very merry, for entirely different reasons, and Crump insisted upon treating the Angel as a "dorg" of the highest degree.

2

After the Angel had left Crump's house he went up the hill again towards the Vicarage. But – possibly moved by the desire to avoid Mrs Gustick – he turned aside at the stile and made a detour by the Lark's Field and Bradley's Farm.

He came upon the Respectable Tramp slumbering peacefully among the wild flowers. He stopped to look, struck by the celestial tranquillity of that individual's face. And even as he did so the Respectable Tramp awoke with a start and sat up. He was a pallid creature, dressed in rusty black, with a broken-spirited crush hat cocked over one eye. "Good afternoon," he said affably. "How are you?"

"Very well, thank you," said the Angel, who had mastered the phrase.

The Respectable Tramp eyed the Angel critically. "Padding the Hoof, matey?" he said. "Like me."

The Angel was puzzled by him. "Why," asked the Angel, "do you sleep like this instead of sleeping up in the air on a Bed?"

"Well I'm blowed!" said the Respectable Tramp. "Why don't I sleep in a bed? Well, it's like this. Sandringham's got the painters in, there's the drains up in Windsor Castle, and I 'aven't no other 'ouse to go to. You 'aven't the price of a arf pint in your pocket, 'ave yer?"

"I have nothing in my pocket," said the Angel.

"Is this here village called Siddermorton?" said the Tramp, rising creakily to his feet and pointing to the clustering roofs down the hill.

"Yes," said the Angel, "they call it Siddermorton."

"I know it, I know it," said the Tramp. "And a very pretty little village it is too." He stretched and yawned, and stood regarding the place.

" 'Ouses," he said reflectively; "Projuce" – waving his hand at the cornfields and orchards. "Looks cosy, don't it?"

"It has a quaint beauty of its own," said the Angel.

"It 'as a quaint beauty of its own – yes... Lord! I'd like to sack the blooming place... I was born there."

"Dear me," said the Angel.

"Yes, I was born there. Ever heard of a pithed frog?"

"Pithed frog," said the Angel. "No!"

"It's a thing these here vivisectionists do. They takes a frog and they cuts out his brains and they shoves a bit of pith in the place of 'em. That's a pithed frog. Well – that there village is full of pithed human beings."

The Angel took it quite seriously. "Is that so?" he said.

"That's so – you take my word for it. Everyone of them 'as 'ad their brains cut out and chunks of rotten touchwood put in the place of it. And you see that little red place there?"

"That's called the national school," said the Angel.

"Yes – that's where they piths 'em," said the Tramp, quite in love with his conceit.

"Really! That's very interesting."

"It stands to reason," said the Tramp. "If they 'ad brains they'd 'ave ideas, and if they 'ad ideas they'd think for themselves. And you can go through that village from end to end and never meet anybody doing as much. Pithed human beings they are. I know that village. I was born there, and I might be there now, a toilin' for my betters, if I 'adnt struck against the pithin'."

"Is it a painful operation?" asked the Angel.

"In parts. Though it aint the heads gets hurt. And it lasts a long time. They take 'em young into that school, and they says to them, 'come in 'ere and we'll improve your minds,' they says, and in the little kiddies go as good as gold. And they begins shovin' it into them. Bit by bit and 'ard and dry, shovin' out the nice juicy brains. Dates and lists and things. Out they comes, no brains in their 'eads, and wound up nice and tight, ready to touch their 'ats to anyone who looks at them. Why! One touched 'is 'at to me yesterday. And they runs about spry and does all the dirty work, and feels thankful they're allowed to live. They take a positive pride in 'ard work for its own sake. Arter they bin pithed. See that chap ploughin'?"

"Yes," said the Angel; "is *he* pithed?"

"Rather. Else he'd be paddin' the hoof this pleasant weather – like me and the blessed Apostles."

"I begin to understand," said the Angel, rather dubiously.

"I knew you would," said the Philosophical Tramp. "I thought you was the right sort. But speaking serious, aint it ridiculous? – centuries and centuries of civilisation, and look at that poor swine there, sweatin' 'isself empty and trudging up that 'ill-side. 'E's English, 'e is. 'E belongs to the top race in creation, 'e does. 'E's one of the rulers of Indjer. It's enough to make a nigger laugh. The flag that's braved a thousand years the battle an' the breeze – that's '*is* flag. There never was a country was as great and glorious as this. Never. And that's wot it makes of us. I'll tell you a little story about them parts as you seems to be a bit of a stranger. There's a chap called Gotch, Sir John Gotch they calls 'im, and when '*e* was a young gent from Oxford, I was a little chap of eight and my sister was a girl of seventeen. Their servant she was. But Lord! everybody's 'eard that story – it's common enough, of 'im or the likes of 'im."

"I haven't," said the Angel.

"All that's pretty and lively of the gals they chucks into the gutters, and all the men with a pennorth of spunk or adventure, all who won't drink what the Curate's wife sends 'em instead of beer, and touch their hats promiscous, and leave the rabbits and birds alone for their betters, gets drove out of the villages as rough characters. Patriotism! Talk about improvin' the race!

Wot's left aint fit to look a nigger in the face, a Chinaman 'ud be ashamed of 'em..."

"But I don't understand," said the Angel. "I don't follow you."

At that the Philosophic Tramp became more explicit, and told the Angel the simple story of Sir John Gotch and the kitchen-maid. It's scarcely necessary to repeat it. You may understand that it left the Angel puzzled. It was full of words he did not understand, for the only vehicle of emotion the Tramp possessed was blasphemy. Yet, though their tongues differed so, he could still convey to the Angel some of his own (probably unfounded) persuasion of the injustice and cruelty of life, and of the utter detestableness of Sir John Gotch.

The last the Angel saw of him was his dusty black back receding down the lane towards Iping Hanger. A pheasant appeared by the roadside, and the Philosophical Tramp immediately caught up a stone and sent the bird clucking with a viciously accurate shot. Then he disappeared round the corner.

CHAPTER FIFTEEN

Mrs Jehoram's Breadth of View

"I heard someone playing the fiddle in the Vicarage, as I came by," said Mrs Jehoram, taking her cup of tea from Mrs Mendham.

"The Vicar plays," said Mrs Mendham. "I have spoken to George about it, but it's no good. I do not think a Vicar should be allowed to do such things. It's so foreign. But there, *he*..."

"I know, dear," said Mrs Jehoram. "But I heard the Vicar once at the schoolroom. I don't think this *was* the Vicar. It was quite clever, some of it, quite smart, you know. And new. I was telling dear Lady Hamergallow this morning. I fancy – "

"The lunatic! Very likely. These half-witted people... My dear, I don't think I shall ever forget that dreadful encounter. Yesterday."

"Nor I."

"My poor girls! They are too shocked to say a word about it. I was telling dear Lady Ham – "

"Quite proper of them. It was *dreadful*, dear. For them."

"And now, dear, I want you to tell me frankly – Do you really believe that creature was a man?"

"You should have heard the violin."

"I still more than half suspect, Jessie – " Mrs Mendham leant forward as if to whisper.

Mrs Jehoram helped herself to cake. "I'm sure no woman could play the violin quite like I heard it played this morning."

"Of course, if you say so that settles the matter," said Mrs Mendham. Mrs Jehoram was the autocratic authority in Siddermorton upon all questions of art, music and belles-lettres. Her late husband had been a minor poet. Then Mrs Mendham added a judicial "Still – "

"Do you know," said Mrs Jehoram, "I'm half inclined to believe the dear Vicar's story."

"How *good* of you, Jessie," said Mrs Mendham.

"But really, I don't think he *could* have had anyone in the Vicarage before that afternoon. I feel sure we should have heard of it. I don't see how a strange cart could come within four miles of Siddermorton without the report coming round to us. The people here gossip so…"

"I always distrust the Vicar," said Mrs Mendham. "I know him."

"Yes. But the story is plausible. If this Mr Angel were someone very clever and eccentric – "

"He would have to be *very* eccentric to dress as he did. There are degrees and limits, dear."

"But kilts," said Mrs Jehoram.

"Are all very well in the Highlands…"

Mrs Jehoram's eyes had rested upon a black speck creeping slowly across a patch of yellowish-green up the hill.

"There he goes," said Mrs Jehoram, rising, "across the cornfield. I'm sure that's him. I can see the hump. Unless it's a man with a sack. Bless me, Minnie! here's an opera glass. How convenient for peeping at the Vicarage!... Yes, it's the man. He is a man. With such a sweet face."

Very unselfishly she allowed her hostess to share the opera glass. For a minute there was a rustling silence.

"His dress," said Mrs Mendham, "is *quite* respectable now."

"Quite," said Mrs Jehoram.

Pause.

"He looks cross!"

"And his coat is dusty."

"He walks steadily enough," said Mrs Mendham, "or one might think... This hot weather..."

Another pause.

"You see, dear," said Mrs Jehoram, putting down the lorgnette. "What I was going to say was, that possibly he might be a genius in disguise."

"If you can call next door to nothing a disguise."

"No doubt it was eccentric. But I've seen children in little blouses, not at all unlike him. So many clever people *are* peculiar in their dress and manners. A genius may steal a horse where a bank-clerk may not look over the hedge. Very possibly he's quite well known and laughing at our Arcadian simplicity. And really it wasn't so improper as some of these New Women bicycling costumes. I saw one in one of the Illustrated Papers only a few days ago – the *New Budget* I think – quite tights, you know, dear. No – I cling to the genius theory. Especially after the playing. I'm sure the creature is original. Perhaps very amusing. In fact, I intend to ask the Vicar to introduce me."

"My dear!" cried Mrs Mendham.

"I'm resolute," said Mrs Jehoram.

"I'm afraid you're rash," said Mrs Mendham. "Geniuses and people of that kind are all very well in London. But here – at the Vicarage."

"We are going to educate the folks. I love originality. At any rate I mean to see him."

"Take care you don't see too much of him," said Mrs Mendham. "I've heard the fashion is quite changing. I understand that some of the very best people have decided that genius is not to be encouraged any more. These recent scandals…"

"Only in literature, I can assure you, dear. In music…"

"Nothing you can say, my dear," said Mrs Mendham, going off at a tangent, "will convince me that that person's costume was not extremely suggestive and improper."

CHAPTER SIXTEEN

A Trivial Incident

The Angel came thoughtfully by the hedge across the field towards the Vicarage. The rays of the setting sun shone on his shoulders, and touched the Vicarage with gold, and blazed like fire in all the windows. By the gate, bathed in the sunlight, stood little Delia, the waiting maid. She stood watching him under her hand. It suddenly came into the Angel's mind that she, at least, was beautiful, and not only beautiful but alive and warm.

She opened the gate for him and stood aside. She was sorry for him, for her elder sister was a cripple. He bowed to her, as he would have done to any woman, and for just one moment looked into her face. She looked back at him and something leapt within her.

The Angel made an irresolute movement. "Your eyes are very beautiful," he said quietly, with a remote wonder in his voice.

"Oh, sir!" she said, starting back. The Angel's expression changed to perplexity. He went on up the pathway between the Vicar's flower-beds, and she stood with the gate held open in her hand, staring after him. Just under the rose-twined verandah he turned and looked at her.

She still stared at him for a moment, and then with a queer gesture turned round with her back to him, shutting the gate as she did so, and seemed to be looking down the valley towards the church tower.

CHAPTER SEVENTEEN

The Warp and the Woof of Things

A t the dinner table the Angel told the Vicar the more striking of his day's adventures.

"The strange thing," said the Angel, "is the readiness of you Human Beings – the zest, with which you inflict pain. Those boys pelting me this morning – "

"Seemed to enjoy it," said the Vicar. "I know."

"Yet they don't like pain," said the Angel.

"No," said the Vicar; "*they* don't like it."

"Then," said the Angel, "I saw some beautiful plants rising with a spike of leaves, two this way and two that, and when I caressed one it caused the most uncomfortable – "

"Stinging nettle!" said the Vicar.

"At any rate a new sort of pain. And another plant with a head like a coronet, and richly decorated leaves, spiked and jagged – "

"A thistle, possibly."

"And in your garden, the beautiful, sweet-smelling plant – "

"The sweet briar," said the Vicar. "I remember."

"And that pink flower that sprang out of the box – "

"Out of the box?" said the Vicar.

"Last night," said the Angel, "that went climbing up the curtains – Flame!"

"Oh! – the matches and the candles! Yes," said the Vicar.

"Then the animals. A dog today behaved most disagreeably – . And these boys, and the way in which people speak – . Everyone seems anxious – willing at any rate – to give this Pain. Everyone seems busy giving pain – "

"Or avoiding it," said the Vicar, pushing his dinner away before him. "Yes – of course. It's fighting everywhere. The whole living world is a battlefield – the whole world. We are driven by Pain. Here. How it lies on the surface! This Angel sees it in a day!"

"But why does everyone – everything – want to give pain?" asked the Angel.

"It is not so in the Angelic Land?" said the Vicar.

"No," said the Angel. "Why is it so here?"

The Vicar wiped his lips with his napkin slowly. "It *is* so," he said. "Pain," said he still more slowly, "is the warp and the woof of this life. Do you know," he said, after a pause, "it is almost impossible for me to imagine...a world without pain... And yet, as you played this morning –

"But this world is different. It is the very reverse of an Angelic world. Indeed, a number of people – excellent religious people – have been so impressed by the universality of pain that they think, after death, things will be even worse for a great many of us. It seems to me an excessive view. But it's a deep question. Almost beyond one's power of discussion – "

And incontinently the Vicar plumped into an impromptu dissertation upon "Necessity," how things were so because they were so, how one *had* to do this and that. "Even our food," said

108

the Vicar. "What?" said the Angel. "Is not obtained without inflicting Pain," said the Vicar.

The Angel's face went so white that the Vicar checked himself suddenly. Or he was just on the very verge of a concise explanation of the antecedents of a leg of lamb. There was a pause.

"By-the-bye," said the Angel, suddenly. "Have you been pithed? Like the common people."

CHAPTER EIGHTEEN

The Angel's Debut

When Lady Hammergallow made up her mind, things happened as she resolved. And though the Vicar made a spasmodic protest, she carried out her purpose and got audience, Angel, and violin together, at Siddermorton House before the week was out. "A genius the Vicar has discovered," she said; so with eminent foresight putting any possibility of blame for a failure on the Vicar's shoulders. "The dear Vicar tells me," she would say, and proceed to marvellous anecdotes of the Angel's cleverness with his instrument. But she was quite in love with her idea – she had always had a secret desire to play the patroness to obscure talent. Hitherto it had not turned out to be talent when it came to the test.

"It would be such a good thing for him," she said. "His hair is long already, and with that high colour he would be beautiful, simply beautiful on a platform. The Vicar's clothes fitting him so badly makes him look quite like a fashionable pianist already. And the scandal of his birth – not told, of course, but whispered – would be – quite an Inducement – when he gets to London, that is."

111

The Vicar had the most horrible sensations as the day approached. He spent hours trying to explain the situation to the Angel, other hours trying to imagine what people would think, still worse hours trying to anticipate the Angel's behaviour. Hitherto the Angel had always played for his own satisfaction. The Vicar would startle him every now and then by rushing upon him with some new point of etiquette that had just occurred to him. As for instance: "It's very important where you put your hat, you know. Don't put it on a chair, whatever you do. Hold it until you get your tea, you know, and then – let me see – then put it down somewhere, you know." The journey to Siddermorton House was accomplished without misadventure, but at the moment of introduction the Vicar had a spasm of horrible misgivings. He had forgotten to explain introductions. The Angel's naïve amusement was evident, but nothing very terrible happened.

"Rummy looking greaser," said Mr Rathbone Slater, who devoted considerable attention to costume. "Wants grooming. No manners. Grinned when he saw me shaking hands. Did it *chic* enough, I thought."

One trivial misadventure occurred. When Lady Hammergallow welcomed the Angel she looked at him through her glasses. The apparent size of her eyes startled him. His surprise and his quick attempt to peer over the brims was only too evident. But the Vicar had warned him of the ear trumpet.

The Angel's incapacity to sit on anything but a music stool appeared to excite some interest among the ladies, but led to no remarks. They regarded it perhaps as the affectation of a budding professional. He was remiss with the teacups and scattered the crumbs of his cake abroad. (You must remember he

112

was quite an amateur at eating.) He crossed his legs. He fumbled over the hat business after vainly trying to catch the Vicar's eye. The eldest Miss Papaver tried to talk to him about continental watering places and cigarettes, and formed a low opinion of his intelligence.

The Angel was surprised by the production of an easel and several books of music, and a little unnerved at first by the sight of Lady Hammergallow sitting with her head on one side, watching him with those magnified eyes through her gilt glasses.

Mrs Jehoram came up to him before he began to play and asked him the Name of the Charming Piece he was playing the other afternoon. The Angel said it had no name, and Mrs Jehoram thought music ought never to have any names and wanted to know who it was by, and when the Angel told her he played it out of his head, she said he must be Quite a Genius and looked open (and indisputably fascinating) admiration at him. The Curate from Iping Hanger (who was professionally a Kelt and who played the piano and talked colour and music with an air of racial superiority) watched him jealously.

The Vicar, who was presently captured and set down next to Lady Hammergallow, kept an anxious eye ever Angelward while she told him particulars of the incomes made by violinists – particulars which, for the most part, she invented as she went along. She had been a little ruffled by the incident of the glasses, but had decided that it came within the limits of permissible originality.

So figure to yourself the Green Saloon at Siddermorton Park; an Angel thinly disguised in clerical vestments and with a violin in his hands, standing by the grand piano, and a respectable gathering of quiet nice people, nicely dressed, grouped about the room. Anticipatory gabble – one hears scattered fragments of conversation.

"He is *incog.*"; said the very eldest Miss Papaver to Mrs Pirbright. "Isn't it quaint and delicious. Jessica Jehoram says she saw him at Vienna, but she can't remember the name. The Vicar knows all about him, but he is so close – "

"How hot and uncomfortable the dear Vicar is looking," said Mrs Pirbright. "I've noticed it before when he sits next to Lady Hammergallow. She simply will *not* respect his cloth. She goes on – "

"His tie is all askew," said the very eldest Miss Papaver, "and his hair! It really hardly looks as though he had brushed it all day."

"Seems a foreign sort of chap. Affected. All very well in a drawing-room," said George Harringay, sitting apart with the younger Miss Pirbright. "But for my part give me a masculine man and a feminine woman. What do you think?"

"Oh! – I think so too," said the younger Miss Pirbright.

"Guineas and guineas," said Lady Hammergallow. "I've heard that some of them keep quite stylish establishments. You would scarcely credit it – "

"I love music, Mr Angel, I adore it. It stirs something in me. I can scarcely describe it," said Mrs Jehoram. "Who is it says that delicious antithesis: Life without music is brutality; music without life is – Dear me! perhaps you remember? Music without life – it's Ruskin I think?"

"I'm sorry that I do not," said the Angel. "I have read very few books."

"How charming of you!" said Mrs Jehoram. "I wish I didn't. I sympathise with you profoundly. I would do the same, only we poor women – I suppose it's originality we lack – And down here one is driven to the most desperate proceedings – "

"He's certainly very *pretty*. But the ultimate test of a man is his strength," said George Harringay. "What do you think?"

"Oh! – I think so too," said the younger Miss Pirbright.

"It's the effeminate man who makes the masculine woman. When the glory of a man is his hair, what's a woman to do? And when men go running about with beautiful hectic dabs – "

"Oh George! You are so dreadfully satirical today," said the younger Miss Pirbright. "I'm *sure* it isn't paint."

"I'm really not his guardian, my dear Lady Hammergallow. Of course it's very kind indeed of you to take such an interest – "

"Are you really going to improvise?" said Mrs Jehoram in a state of cooing delight.

"*SSsh*!" said the curate from Iping Hanger.

Then the Angel began to play, looking straight before him as he did so, thinking of the wonderful things of the Angelic Land, and yet insensibly letting the sadness he was beginning to feel, steal over the fantasia he was playing. When he forgot his company the music was strange and sweet; when the sense of his surroundings floated into his mind the music grew capricious and grotesque. But so great was the hold of the Angelic music upon the Vicar that his anxieties fell from him at once, so soon as the Angel began to play. Mrs Jehoram sat and looked rapt and sympathetic as hard as she could (though the music was puzzling at times) and tried to catch the Angel's eye. He really had a wonderfully mobile face, and the tenderest shades of expression! And Mrs Jehoram was a judge. George Harringay looked bored, until the younger Miss Pirbright, who adored him, put out her mousy little shoe to touch his manly boot, and then he turned his face to catch the feminine delicacy of her coquettish eye, and was comforted. The very eldest Miss Papaver and Mrs Pirbright sat quite still and looked churchy for nearly four minutes.

Then said the eldest Miss Papaver in a whisper, "I always Enjoy violin music so much." And Mrs Pirbright answered, "We get so little Nice music down here." And Miss Papaver said, "He plays Very nicely." And Mrs Pirbright, "Such a Delicate Touch!" And Miss Papaver, "Does Willie keep up his lessons?" and so to a whispered conversation.

The Curate from Iping Hanger sat (he felt) in full view of the company. He had one hand curled round his ear, and his eyes hard and staring fixedly at the pedestal of the Hammergallow Sèvres vase. He supplied, by the movements of his mouth, a kind of critical guide to any of the company who were disposed to avail themselves of it. It was a generous way he had. His aspect was severely judicial, tempered by starts of evident disapproval and guarded appreciation. The Vicar leaned back in his chair and stared at the Angel's face, and was presently rapt away in a wonderful dream. Lady Hammergallow, with quick jerky movements of the head and a low but insistent rustling, surveyed and tried to judge of the effect of the Angelic playing. Mr Rathbone-Slater stared very solemnly into his hat and looked very miserable, and Mrs Rathbone-Slater made mental memoranda of Mrs Jehoram's sleeves. And the air about them all was heavy with exquisite music – for all that had ears to hear.

"Scarcely affected enough," whispered Lady Hammergallow hoarsely, suddenly poking the Vicar in the ribs. The Vicar came out of Dreamland suddenly. "Eigh?" shouted the Vicar, startled, coming up with a jump. "Sssh!" said the Curate from Iping Hanger, and everyone looked shocked at the brutal insensibility

116

of Hilyer. "So unusual of the Vicar," said the very eldest Miss Papaver, "to do things like that!" The Angel went on playing.

The Curate from Iping Hanger began making mesmeric movements with his index finger, and as the thing proceeded Mr Rathbone-Slater got amazingly limp. He solemnly turned his hat round and altered his view. The Vicar lapsed from an uneasy discomfort into dreamland again. Lady Hammergallow rustled a great deal, and presently found a way of making her chair creak. And at last the thing came to an end. Lady Hammergallow exclaimed "De – licious!" though she had never heard a note, and began clapping her hands. At that everyone clapped except Mr Rathbone-Slater, who rapped his hat brim instead. The Curate from Iping Hanger clapped with a judicial air.

"So I said (*clap, clap, clap*), if you cannot cook the food my way (*clap, clap, clap*) you must *go*," said Mrs Pirbright, clapping vigorously. "(This music is a delightful treat.)"

"(It is. I always *revel* in music,)" said the very eldest Miss Papaver. "And did she improve after that?"

"Not a bit of it," said Mrs Pirbright.

The Vicar woke up again and stared round the saloon. Did other people see these visions, or were they confined to him alone? Surely they must all see...and have a wonderful command of their feelings. It was incredible that such music should not affect them. "He's a trifle *gauche*," said Lady Hammergallow, jumping upon the Vicar's attention. "He neither bows nor smiles. He must cultivate oddities like that. Every successful executant is more or less *gauche*."

"Did you really make that up yourself?" said Mrs Jehoram, sparkling her eyes at him, "as you went along. Really, it is *wonderful*! Nothing less than wonderful."

"A little amateurish," said the Curate from Iping Hanger to Mr Rathbone-Slater. "A great gift, undoubtedly, but a certain lack of sustained training. There were one or two little things... I would like to talk to him."

"His trousers look like concertinas," said Mr Rathbone-Slater. "He ought to be told *that*. It's scarcely decent."

"Can you do Imitations, Mr Angel?" said Lady Hammergallow.

"Oh *do*, do some Imitations!" said Mrs Jehoram. "I adore Imitations."

"It was a fantastic thing," said the Curate of Iping Hanger to the Vicar of Siddermorton, waving his long indisputably musical hands as he spoke; "a little involved, to my mind. I have heard it before somewhere – I forget where. He has genius undoubtedly, but occasionally he is – loose. There is a certain deadly precision wanting. There are years of discipline yet."

"I *don't* admire these complicated pieces of music," said George Harringay. "I have simple tastes, I'm afraid. There seems to me no *tune* in it. There's nothing I like so much as simple music. Tune, simplicity is the need of the age, in my opinion. We are so over subtle. Everything is far-fetched. Home-grown thoughts and 'Home, Sweet Home' for me. What do you think?"

"Oh! I think so – *quite*," said the younger Miss Pirbright.

"Well, Amy, chattering to George as usual?" said Mrs Pirbright, across the room.

"As usual, Ma!" said the younger Miss Pirbright, glancing round with a bright smile at Miss Papaver, and turning again so as not to lose the next utterance from George.

"I wonder if you and Mr Angel could manage a duet?" said Lady Hammergallow to the Curate from Iping Hanger, who was looking preternaturally gloomy.

"I'm sure I should be delighted," said the Curate from Iping Hanger, brightening up.

"Duets!" said the Angel; "the two of us. Then he can play. I understood – the Vicar told me – "

"Mr Wilmerdings is an accomplished pianist," interrupted the Vicar.

"But the Imitations?" said Mrs Jehoram, who detested Wildermings.

"Imitations!" said the Angel.

"A pig squeaking, a cock crowing, you know," said Mr Rathbone-Slater, and added lower, "Best fun you can get out of a fiddle – *my* opinion."

"I really don't understand," said the Angel. "A pig crowing!"

"You don't like Imitations," said Mrs Jehoram. "Nor do I – really. I accept the snub. I think they degrade..."

"Perhaps afterwards Mr Angel will Relent," said Lady Hammergallow, when Mrs Pirbright had explained the matter to her. She could scarcely credit her ear trumpet. When she asked for Imitations she was accustomed to get Imitations.

Mr Wilmerdings had seated himself at the piano, and had turned to a familiar pile of music in the recess. "What do you think of that Barcarole thing of Spohr's?" he said over his shoulder. "I suppose you know it?" The Angel looked bewildered.

He opened the folio before the Angel.

"What an odd kind of book!" said the Angel. "What do all those crazy dots mean?" (At that the Vicar's blood ran cold.)

"What dots?" said the Curate.

"There!" said the Angel with incriminating finger.

"Oh *come!*" said the Curate.

There was one of those swift, short silences that mean so much in a social gathering.

Then the eldest Miss Papaver turned upon the Vicar. "Does not Mr Angel play from ordinary... Music – from the ordinary notation?"

"I have never heard," said the Vicar, getting red now after the first shock of horror. "I have really never seen..."

The Angel felt the situation was strained, though what was straining it he could not understand. He became aware of a doubtful, an unfriendly look upon the faces that regarded him. "Impossible!" he heard Mrs Pirbright say; "after that *beautiful* music." The eldest Miss Papaver went to Lady Hammergallow at once, and began to explain into her ear trumpet that Mr Angel did not wish to play with Mr Wilmerdings, and alleged an ignorance of written music.

"He cannot play from Notes!" said Lady Hammergallow in a voice of measured horror. "Non – sense!"

"Notes!" said the Angel perplexed. "Are these notes?"

"It's carrying the joke too far – simply because he doesn't want to play with Wilmerdings," said Mr Rathbone-Slater to George Harringay.

There was an expectant pause. The Angel perceived he had to be ashamed of himself. He was ashamed of himself.

"Then," said Lady Hammergallow, throwing her head back and speaking with deliberate indignation, as she rustled forward, "if you cannot play with Mr Wilmerdings I am afraid I cannot ask you to play again." She made it sound like an ultimatum. Her glasses in her hand quivered violently with indignation. The

Angel was now human enough to appreciate the fact that he was crushed.

"What is it?" said little Lucy Rustchuck in the further bay.

"He's refused to play with old Wilmerdings," said Tommy Rathbone-Slater. "What a lark! The old girl's purple. She thinks heaps of that ass, Wilmerdings."

"Perhaps, Mr Wilmerdings, you will favour us with that delicious Polonaise of Chopin's," said Lady Hammergallow. Everybody else was hushed. The indignation of Lady Hammergallow inspired much the same silence as a coming earthquake or an eclipse. Mr Wilmerdings perceived he would be doing a real social service to begin at once, and (be it entered to his credit now that his account draws near its settlement) he did.

"If a man pretend to practise an Art," said George Harringay, "he ought at least to have the conscience to study the elements of it. What do you..."

"Oh! I think so too," said the younger Miss Pirbright.

The Vicar felt that the heavens had fallen. He sat crumpled up in his chair, a shattered man. Lady Hammergallow sat down next to him without appearing to see him. She was breathing heavily, but her face was terribly calm. Everyone sat down. Was the Angel grossly ignorant or only grossly impertinent? The Angel was vaguely aware of some frightful offence, aware that in some mysterious way he had ceased to be the centre of the gathering. He saw reproachful despair in the Vicar's eye. He drifted slowly towards the window in the recess and sat down on the little octagonal Moorish stool by the side of Mrs Jehoram. And under the circumstances he appreciated at more than its proper value Mrs Jehoram's kindly smile. He put down the violin in the window seat.

121

2

Mrs Jehoram and the Angel (apart) – Mr Wilmerdings playing.

"I have so longed for a quiet word with you," said Mrs Jehoram in a low tone. "To tell you how delightful I found your playing."

"I am glad it pleased you," said the Angel.

"Pleased is scarcely the word," said Mrs Jehoram. "I was moved – profoundly. These others did not understand... I was glad you did not play with him."

The Angel looked at the mechanism called Wilmerdings, and felt glad too. (The Angelic conception of duets is a kind of conversation upon violins.) But he said nothing.

"I worship music," said Mrs Jehoram. "I know nothing about it technically, but there is something in it – a longing, a wish..."

The Angel stared at her face. She met his eyes.

"You understand," she said. "I see you understand." He was certainly a very nice boy, sentimentally precocious perhaps, and with deliciously liquid eyes.

There was an interval of Chopin (Op. 40) played with immense precision.

Mrs Jehoram had a sweet face still, in shadow, with the light falling round her golden hair, and a curious theory flashed across the Angel's mind. The perceptible powder only supported his view of something infinitely bright and lovable caught, tarnished, coarsened, coated over.

"Do you," said the Angel in a low tone. "Are you...separated from...*your* world?"

"As you are?" whispered Mrs Jehoram.

"This is so – cold," said the Angel. "So harsh!" He meant the whole world.

"I feel it too," said Mrs Jehoram, referring to Siddermorton Home.

"There are those who cannot live without sympathy," she said after a sympathetic pause. "And times when one feels alone in the world. Fighting a battle against it all. Laughing, flirting, hiding the pain of it…"

"And hoping," said the Angel with a wonderful glance. – "Yes."

Mrs Jehoram (who was an epicure of flirtations) felt the Angel was more than redeeming the promise of his appearance. (Indisputably he worshipped her.) "Do *you* look for sympathy?" she said. "Or have you found it?"

"I think," said the Angel, very softly, leaning forward, "I think I have found it."

Interval of Chopin Op. 40. The very eldest Miss Papaver and Mrs Pirbright whispering. Lady Hammergallow (glasses up) looking down the saloon with an unfriendly expression at the Angel. Mrs Jehoram and the Angel exchanging deep and significant glances.

"Her name," said the Angel (Mrs Jehoram made a movement) "is Delia. She is…"

"Delia!" said Mrs Jehoram sharply, slowly realising a terrible misunderstanding. "A fanciful name… Why!… No! Not that little housemaid at the Vicarage – ?…"

The Polonaise terminated with a flourish. The Angel was quite surprised at the change in Mrs Jehoram's expression.

123

"I *never* did!" said Mrs Jehoram recovering. "To make me your confidant in an intrigue with a servant. Really Mr Angel it's possible to be too original..."

Then suddenly their colloquy was interrupted.

3

This section is (so far as my memory goes) the shortest in the book.

But the enormity of the offence necessitates the separation of this section from all other sections.

The Vicar, you must understand, had done his best to inculcate the recognised differentiae of a gentleman. "Never allow a lady to carry anything," said the Vicar. "Say, 'permit me' and relieve her." "Always stand until every lady is seated." "Always rise and open a door for a lady..." and so forth. (All men who have elder sisters know that code.)

And the Angel (who had failed to relieve Lady Hammergallow of her teacup) danced forward with astonishing dexterity (leaving Mrs Jehoram in the window seat) and with an elegant "permit me" rescued the tea-tray from Lady Hammergallow's pretty parlour-maid and vanished officiously in front of her. The Vicar rose to his feet with an inarticulate cry.

4

"He's drunk!" said Mr Rathbone-Slater, breaking a terrific silence. "That's the matter with him."

Mrs Jehoram laughed hysterically.

The Vicar stood up, motionless, staring. "Oh! I *forgot* to explain servants to him!" said the Vicar to himself in a swift outbreak of remorse. "I thought he *did* understand servants."

"Really, Mr Hilyer!" said Lady Hammergallow, evidently exercising enormous self-control and speaking in panting spasms. "Really, Mr Hilyer! – Your genius is *too* terrible. I must, I really *must*, ask you to take him home."

So to the dialogue in the corridor of alarmed maid-servant and well-meaning (but shockingly *gauche*) Angel – appears the Vicar, his botryoidal little face crimson, gaunt despair in his eyes, and his necktie under his left ear.

"Come," he said – struggling with emotion. "Come away... I... I am disgraced for ever."

And the Angel stared for a second at him and obeyed – meekly, perceiving himself in the presence of unknown but evidently terrible forces.

And so began and ended the Angel's social career.

In the informal indignation meeting that followed, Lady Hammergallow took the (informal) chair. "I feel humiliated," she said. "The Vicar assured me he was an exquisite player. I never imagined..."

"He was drunk," said Mr Rathbone-Slater. "You could tell it from the way he fumbled with his tea."

"Such a *fiasco*!" said Mrs Mergle.

"The Vicar assured me," said Lady Hammergallow. " 'The man I have staying with me is a musical genius,' he said. His very words."

"His ears must be burning anyhow," said Tommy Rathbone-Slater.

125

"I was trying to keep him Quiet," said Mrs Jehoram. "By humouring him. And do you know the things he said to me – there!"

"The thing he played," said Mr Wilmerdings, " – I must confess I did not like to charge him to his face. But really! It was merely *drifting*."

"Just fooling with a fiddle, eigh?" said George Harringay. "Well I thought it was beyond me. So much of your fine music is – "

"Oh, *George*!" said the younger Miss Pirbright.

"The Vicar was a bit on too – to judge by his tie," said Mr Rathbone-Slater. "It's a dashed rummy go. Did you notice how he fussed after the genius?"

"One has to be so very careful," said the very eldest Miss Papaver.

"He told me he is in love with the Vicar's housemaid!" said Mrs Jehoram. "I almost laughed in his face."

"The Vicar ought *never* to have brought him here," said Mrs Rathbone-Slater with decision.

Chapter Nineteen

The Trouble of the Barbed Wire

So, ingloriously, ended the Angel's first and last appearance in Society. Vicar and Angel returned to the Vicarage; crestfallen black figures in the bright sunlight, going dejectedly. The Angel, deeply pained that the Vicar was pained. The Vicar, dishevelled and desperate, intercalating spasmodic remorse and apprehension with broken explanations of the Theory of Etiquette. "They do not understand," said the Vicar over and over again. "They will all be so very much aggrieved. I do not know what to say to them. It is all so confused, so perplexing." And at the gate of the Vicarage, at the very spot where Delia had first seemed beautiful, stood Horrocks the village constable, awaiting them. He held coiled up about his hand certain short lengths of barbed wire.

"Good evening, Horrocks," said the Vicar as the constable held the gate open.

"Evenin', Sir," said Horrocks, and added in a kind of mysterious undertone, "*Could* I speak to you a minute, Sir?"

"Certainly," said the Vicar. The Angel walked on thoughtfully to the house, and meeting Delia in the hall stopped her and cross-examined her at length over differences between Servants and Ladies.

"You'll excuse my taking the liberty, Sir," said Horrocks, "but there's trouble brewin' for that crippled gent you got stayin' here."

"Bless me!" said the Vicar. "You don't say so!"

"Sir John Gotch, Sir. He's very angry indeed, Sir. His language, Sir – . But I felt bound to tell you, Sir. He's certain set on taking out a summons on account of that there barbed wire. Certain set, Sir, he is."

"Sir John Gotch!" said the Vicar. "Wire! I don't understand."

"He asked me to find out who did it. Course I've had to do my duty, Sir. Naturally a disagreeable one."

"Barbed wire! Duty! I don't understand you, Horrocks."

"I'm afraid, Sir, there's no denying the evidence. I've made careful enquiries, Sir." And forthwith the constable began telling the Vicar of a new and terrible outrage committed by the Angelic visitor.

But we need not follow that explanation in detail – or the subsequent confession. (For my own part I think there is nothing more tedious than dialogue.) It gave the Vicar a new view of the Angelic character, a vignette of the Angelic indignation. A shady lane, sun-mottled, sweet hedges full of honeysuckle and vetch on either side, and a little girl gathering flowers, forgetful of the barbed wire which, all along the Sidderford Road, fenced in the dignity of Sir John Gotch from "bounders" and the detested "million." Then suddenly a gashed hand, a bitter outcry, and the Angel sympathetic, comforting, inquisitive. Explanations sob-set, and then – altogether novel phenomenon in the Angelic career – *passion*. A furious onslaught upon the barbed wire of Sir

John Gotch, barbed wire recklessly handled, slashed, bent and broken. Yet the Angel acted without personal malice – saw in the thing only an ugly and vicious plant that trailed insidiously among its fellows. Finally the Angel's explanations gave the Vicar a picture of the Angel alone amidst his destruction, trembling and amazed at the sudden force, not himself, that had sprung up within him, and set him striking and cutting. Amazed, too, at the crimson blood that trickled down his fingers.

"It is still more horrible," said the Angel when the Vicar explained the artificial nature of the thing. "If I had seen the man who put this silly-cruel stuff there to hurt little children, I know I should have tried to inflict pain upon him. I have never felt like this before. I am indeed becoming tainted and coloured altogether by the wickedness of this world."

"To think, too, that you men should be so foolish as to uphold the laws that let a man do such spiteful things. Yes – I know; you will say it has to be so. For some remoter reason. That is a thing that only makes me angrier. Why cannot an act rest on its own merits?... As it does in the Angelic Land."

That was the incident the history of which the Vicar now gradually learnt, getting the bare outline from Horrocks, the colour and emotion subsequently from the Angel. The thing had happened the day before the musical festival at Siddermorton House.

"Have you told Sir John who did it?" asked the Vicar. "And are you sure?"

"Quite sure, Sir. There can be no doubting it was your gentleman, Sir. I've not told Sir John yet, Sir. But I shall have to tell Sir John this evening. Meaning no offence to you, Sir, as I hopes you'll see. It's my duty, Sir. Besides which – "

129

"Of course," said the Vicar, hastily. "Certainly it's your duty. And what will Sir John do?"

"He's dreadful set against the person who did it – destroying property like that – and sort of slapping his arrangements in the face."

Pause. Horrocks made a movement. The Vicar, tie almost at the back of his neck now, a most unusual thing for him, stared blankly at his toes.

"I thought I'd tell you, Sir," said Horrocks.

"Yes," said the Vicar. "Thanks, Horrocks, thanks!" He scratched the back of his head. "You might perhaps... I think it's the best way... Quite sure Mr Angel did it?"

"Sherlock 'Omes, Sir, couldn't be cocksurer."

"Then I'd better give you a little note to the Squire."

2

The Vicar's table-talk at dinner that night, after the Angel had stated his case, was full of grim explanations, prisons, madness.

"It's too late to tell the truth about you now," said the Vicar. "Besides, that's impossible. I really do not know what to say. We must face our circumstances, I suppose. I am so undecided – so torn. It's the two worlds. If your Angelic world were only a dream, or if *this* world were only a dream – or if I could believe either or both dreams, it would be all right with me. But here is a real Angel and a real summons – how to reconcile them I do not know. I must talk to Gotch... But he won't understand. Nobody will understand..."

"I am putting you to terrible inconvenience, I am afraid. My appalling unworldliness – "

"It's not you," said the Vicar. "It's not you. I perceive you have brought something strange and beautiful into my life. It's not you. It's myself. If I had more faith either way. If I could believe entirely in this world, and call you an Abnormal Phenomenon, as Crump does. But no. Terrestrial Angelic, Angelic Terrestrial... See-Saw.

"Still, Gotch is certain to be disagreeable, *most* disagreeable. He always is. It puts me into his hands. He is a bad moral influence, I know. Drinking. Gambling. Worse. Still, one must render unto Caesar the things that are Caesar's. And he is against Disestablishment..."

Then the Vicar would revert to the social collapse of the afternoon. "You are so very fundamental, you know," he said — several times.

The Angel went to his own room puzzled but very depressed. Every day the world had frowned darker upon him and his angelic ways. He could see how the trouble affected the Vicar, yet he could not imagine how he could avert it. It was all so strange and unreasonable. Twice again, too, he had been pelted out of the village.

He found the violin lying on his bed where he had laid it before dinner. And taking it up he began to play to comfort himself. But now he played no delicious vision of the Angelic Land. The iron of the world was entering into his soul. For a week now he had known pain and rejection, suspicion and hatred; a strange new spirit of revolt was growing up in his heart. He played a melody, still sweet and tender as those of the Angelic Land, but charged with a new note, the note of human sorrow and effort, now swelling into something like defiance, dying now into a plaintive sadness. He played softly, playing to himself to comfort himself, but the Vicar heard, and all his finite bothers were swallowed up in a hazy melancholy, a melancholy that was quite remote from sorrow. And besides the Vicar, the Angel had another hearer of whom neither Angel nor Vicar was thinking.

CHAPTER TWENTY

Delia

She was only four or five yards away from the Angel in the westward gable. The diamond-paned window of her little white room was open. She knelt on her box of japanned tin, and rested her chin on her hands, her elbows on the windowsill. The young moon hung over the pine trees, and its light, cool and colourless, lay softly upon the silent-sleeping world. Its light fell upon her white face, and discovered new depths in her dreaming eyes. Her soft lips fell apart and showed the little white teeth.

Delia was thinking, vaguely, wonderfully, as girls will think. It was feeling rather than thinking; clouds of beautiful translucent emotion drove across the clear sky of her mind, taking shape that changed and vanished. She had all that wonderful emotional tenderness, that subtle exquisite desire for self-sacrifice, which exists so inexplicably in a girl's heart, exists it seems only to be presently trampled under foot by the grim and gross humours of daily life, to be ploughed in again roughly and remorselessly, as the farmer ploughs in the clover that has sprung up in the soil. She had been looking out at the tranquillity of the moonlight long before the Angel began to play, – waiting; then suddenly the quiet, motionless beauty of silver and shadow was suffused with tender music.

She did not move, but her lips closed and her eyes grew even softer. She had been thinking before of the strange glory that had suddenly flashed out about the stooping hunchback when he spoke to her in the sunset; of that and of a dozen other glances, chance turns, even once the touching of her hand. That afternoon he had spoken to her, asking strange questions. Now the music seemed to bring his very face before her, his look of half curious solicitude, peering into her face, into her eyes, into her and through her, deep down into her soul. He seemed now to be speaking directly to her, telling her of his solitude and trouble. Oh! that regret, that longing! For he was in trouble. And how could a servant-girl help him, this soft-spoken gentleman who carried himself so kindly, who played so sweetly. The music was so sweet and keen, it came so near to the thought of her heart, that presently one hand tightened on the other, and the tears came streaming down her face.

As Crump would tell you, people do not do that kind of thing unless there is something wrong with the nervous system. But then, from the scientific point of view, being in love is a pathological condition.

I am painfully aware of the objectionable nature of my story here. I have even thought of wilfully perverting the truth to propitiate the Lady Reader. But I could not. The story has been too much for me. I do the thing with my eyes open. Delia must remain what she really was – a servant girl. I know that to give a mere servant girl, or at least an English servant girl, the refined feelings of a human being, to present her as speaking with anything but an intolerable confusion of aspirates, places me outside the pale of respectable writers. Association with servants, even in thought, is dangerous in these days. I can only plead (pleading vainly, I know), that Delia was a very exceptional servant girl. Possibly, if one enquired, it might be found that her parentage was upper middle-class – that she was made of the finer upper middle-class clay. And (this perhaps may avail me better) I will promise that in some future work I will redress the balance, and the patient reader shall have the recognised article, enormous feet and hands, systematic aspiration of vowels and elimination of aspirates, no figure (only middle-class girls have figures – the thing is beyond a servant-girl's means), a fringe (by agreement), and a cheerful readiness to dispose of her self-respect for half-a-crown. That is the accepted English servant, the typical English woman (when stripped of money and accomplishments) as she appears in the works of contemporary writers. But Delia somehow was different. I can only regret the circumstance – it was altogether beyond my control.

CHAPTER TWENTY-ONE

Doctor Crump Acts

Early the next morning the Angel went down through the village, and climbing the fence, waded through the waist-high reeds that fringe the Sidder. He was going to Bandram Bay to take a nearer view of the sea, which one could just see on a clear day from the higher parts of Siddermorton Park. And suddenly he came upon Crump sitting on a log and smoking. (Crump always smoked exactly two ounces per week – and he always smoked it in the open air.)

"Hullo!" said Crump, in his healthiest tone. "How's the wing?"

"Very well," said the Angel. "The pain's gone."

"I suppose you know you are trespassing?"

"Trespassing!" said the Angel.

"I suppose you don't know what that means," said Crump.

"I don't," said the Angel.

"I must congratulate you. I don't know how long you will last, but you are keeping it up remarkably well. I thought at first you were a mattoid, but you're so amazingly consistent. Your attitude of entire ignorance of the elementary facts of Life is really a very amusing pose. You make slips of course, but very few. But surely we two understand one another."

He smiled at the Angel. "You would beat Sherlock Holmes. I wonder who you really are."

The Angel smiled back, with eyebrows raised and hands extended. "It's impossible for you to know who I am. Your eyes are blind, your ears deaf, your soul dark, to all that is wonderful about me. It's no good my telling that I fell into your world."

The Doctor waved his pipe. "Not that, please. I don't want to pry if you have your reasons for keeping quiet. Only I would like you to think of Hilyer's mental health. He really believes this story."

The Angel shrugged his dwindling wings.

"You did not know him before this affair. He's changed tremendously. He used to be neat and comfortable. For the last fortnight he's been hazy, with a far-away look in his eyes. He preached last Sunday without his cufflinks, and something wrong with his tie, and he took for his text, 'Eye hath not seen nor ear heard.' He really believes all this nonsense about the Angel-land. The man is verging on monomania!"

"You *will* see things from your own standpoint," said the Angel.

"Everyone must. At any rate, I think it jolly regrettable to see this poor old fellow hypnotised, as you certainly have hypnotised him. I don't know where you come from nor who you are, but I warn you I'm not going to see the old boy made a fool of much longer."

"But he's not being made a fool of. He's simply beginning to dream of a world outside his knowledge – "

"It won't do," said Crump. "I'm not one of the dupe class. You are either of two things – a lunatic at large (which I don't believe), or a knave. Nothing else is possible. I think I know a little of this world, whatever I do of yours. Very well. If you don't leave Hilyer alone I shall communicate with the police, and either clap you into a prison, if you go back on your story, or into a madhouse if you don't. It's stretching a point, but I swear I'd certify you insane tomorrow to get you out of the village. It's not only the Vicar. As you know. I hope that's plain. Now what have you to say?"

With an affectation of great calm, the Doctor took out his penknife and began to dig the blade into his pipe bowl. His pipe had gone out during this last speech.

For a moment neither spoke. The Angel looked about him with a face that grew pale. The Doctor extracted a plug of tobacco from his pipe and flung it away, shut his penknife and put it in his waistcoat pocket. He had not meant to speak quite so emphatically, but speech always warmed him.

"Prison," said the Angel. "Madhouse! Let me see." Then he remembered the Vicar's explanation. "Not that!" he said. He approached Crump with eyes dilated and hands outstretched.

"I knew *you* would know what those things meant – at any rate. Sit down," said Crump, indicating the tree trunk beside him by a movement of the head.

The Angel, shivering, sat down on the tree trunk and stared at the Doctor.

Crump was getting out his pouch. "You are a strange man," said the Angel. "Your beliefs are like – a steel trap."

"They are," said Crump – flattered.

"But I tell you – I assure you the thing is so – I know nothing, or at least remember nothing of anything I knew of this world before I found myself in the darkness of night on the moorland above Sidderford."

"Where did you learn the language then?"

"I don't know. Only I tell you – But I haven't an atom of the sort of proof that would convince you."

"And you really," said Crump, suddenly coming round upon him and looking into his eyes; "You really believe you were eternally in a kind of glorious heaven before then?"

"I do," said the Angel.

"Pshaw!" said Crump, and lit his pipe. He sat smoking, elbow on knee, for some time, and the Angel sat and watched him. Then his face grew less troubled.

"It is just possible," he said to himself rather than to the Angel, and began another piece of silence.

"You see," he said, when that was finished. "There is such a thing as double personality... A man sometimes forgets who he is and thinks he is someone else. Leaves home, friends, and everything, and leads a double life. There was a case in *Nature* only a month or so ago. The man was sometimes English and right-handed, and sometimes Welsh and left-handed. When he was English he knew no Welsh, when he was Welsh he knew no English... H'm."

He turned suddenly on the Angel and said "Home!" He fancied he might revive in the Angel some latent memory of his lost youth. He went on "Dadda, Pappa, Daddy, Mammy, Pappy, Father, Dad, Governor, Old Boy, Mother, dear Mother, Ma, Mumsy... No good? What are you laughing at?"

"Nothing," said the Angel. "You surprised me a little, – that is all. A week ago I should have been puzzled by that vocabulary."

For a minute Crump rebuked the Angel silently out of the corner of his eye.

"You have such an ingenuous face. You almost force me to believe you. You are certainly not an ordinary lunatic. Your mind – except for your isolation from the past – seems balanced enough. I wish Nordau or Lombroso or some of these *Saltpetriere* men could have a look at you. Down here one gets no practice worth speaking about in mental cases. There's one idiot – and he's just a damned idiot of an idiot –; all the rest are thoroughly sane people."

"Possibly that accounts for their behaviour," said the Angel thoughtfully.

"But to consider your general position here," said Crump, ignoring his comment, "I really regard you as a bad influence here. These fancies are contagious. It is not simply the Vicar. There is a man named Shine has caught the fad, and he has been in the drink for a week, off and on, and offering to fight anyone who says you are not an Angel. Then a man over at Sidderford is, I hear, affected with a kind of religious mania on the same tack. These things spread. There ought to be a quarantine in mischievous ideas. And I have heard another story..."

"But what can I do?" said the Angel. "Suppose I am (quite unintentionally) doing mischief..."

"You can leave the village," said Crump.

"Then I shall only go into another village."

"That's not my affair," said Crump. "Go where you like. Only go. Leave these three people, the Vicar, Shine, the little servant girl, whose heads are all spinning with galaxies of Angels..."

"But," said the Angel. "Face your world! I tell you I can't. And leave Delia! I don't understand... I do not know how to set about getting Work and Food and Shelter. And I am growing afraid of human beings..."

"Fancies, fancies," said Crump, watching him, "mania."

"It's no good my persisting in worrying you," he said suddenly, "but certainly the situation is impossible as it stands." He stood up with a jerk.

"Good morning, Mr – Angel," he said, "the long and the short of it is – I say it as the medical adviser of this parish – you are an unhealthy influence. We can't have you. You must go."

He turned, and went striding through the grass towards the roadway, leaving the Angel sitting disconsolately on the tree trunk. "An unhealthy influence," said the Angel slowly, staring blankly in front of him, and trying to realise what it meant.

Chapter Twenty-two

Sir John Gotch Acts

Sir John Gotch was a little man with scrubby hair, a small, thin nose sticking out of a face crackled with wrinkles, tight brown gaiters, and a riding whip. "I've come, you see," he said, as Mrs Hinijer closed the door.

"Thank you," said the Vicar, "I'm obliged to you. I'm really obliged to you."

"Glad to be of any service to you," said Sir John Gotch. (Angular attitude.)

"This business," said the Vicar, "this unfortunate business of the barbed wire – is really, you know, a most unfortunate business."

Sir John Gotch became decidedly more angular in his attitude. "It is," he said.

"This Mr Angel being my guest – "

"No reason why he should cut my wire," said Sir John Gotch, briefly.

"None whatever."

"May I ask *who* this Mr Angel is?" asked Sir John Gotch with the abruptness of long premeditation.

143

The Vicar's fingers jumped to his chin. What *was* the good of talking to a man like Sir John Gotch about Angels?

"To tell you the exact truth," said the Vicar, "there is a little secret – "

"Lady Hammergallow told me as much."

The Vicar's face suddenly became bright red.

"Do you know," said Sir John, with scarcely a pause, "he's been going about this village preaching Socialism?"

"Good heavens!" said the Vicar, "*No!*"

"He has. He has been buttonholing every yokel he came across, and asking them why they had to work, while we – I and you, you know – did nothing. He has been saying we ought to educate every man up to your level and mine – out of the rates, I suppose, as usual. He has been suggesting that we – I and you, you know – keep these people down – pith 'em."

"*Dear* me!" said the Vicar, "I had no idea."

"He has done this wire-cutting as a demonstration, I tell you, as a Socialistic demonstration. If we don't come down on him pretty sharply, I tell you, we shall have the palings down in Flinders Lane next, and the next thing will be ricks afire, and every damned (I beg your pardon, Vicar. I know I'm too fond of that word), every blessed pheasant's egg in the parish smashed. I know these – "

"A Socialist," said the Vicar, quite put out, "I had *no* idea."

"You see why I am inclined to push matters against our gentleman though he *is* your guest. It seems to me he has been taking advantage of your paternal – "

"Oh, *not* paternal!" said the Vicar. "Really – "

144

"(I beg your pardon, Vicar – it was a slip.) Of your kindness, to go mischief-making everywhere, setting class against class, and the poor man against his bread and butter."

The Vicar's fingers were at his chin again.

"So there's one of two things," said Sir John Gotch. "Either that Guest of yours leaves the parish, or – I take proceedings. That's final."

The Vicar's mouth was all askew.

"That's the position," said Sir John, jumping to his feet, "if it were not for you, I should take proceedings at once. As it is – am I to take proceedings or no?"

"You see," said the Vicar in horrible perplexity.

"Well?"

"Arrangements have to be made."

"He's a mischief-making idler... I know the breed. But I'll give you a week – "

"Thank you," said the Vicar. "I understand your position. I perceive the situation is getting intolerable..."

"Sorry to give you this bother, of course," said Sir John.

"A week," said the Vicar.

"A week," said Sir John, leaving.

The Vicar returned, after accompanying Gotch out, and for a long time he remained sitting before the desk in his study, plunged in thought. "A week!" he said, after an immense silence. "Here is an Angel, a glorious Angel, who has quickened my soul to beauty and delight, who has opened my eyes to Wonderland, and something more than Wonderland,...and I have promised to get rid of him in a week! What are we men made of?... How *can* I tell him?"

He began to walk up and down the room, then he went into the dining-room, and stood staring blankly out at the cornfield. The table was already laid for lunch. Presently he turned, still dreaming, and almost mechanically helped himself to a glass of sherry.

CHAPTER TWENTY-THREE

The Sea Cliff

The Angel lay upon the summit of the cliff above Bandram Bay, and stared out at the glittering sea. Sheer from under his elbows fell the cliff, five hundred and seven feet of it down to the datum line, and the sea-birds eddied and soared below him. The upper part of the cliff was a greenish chalky rock, the lower two-thirds a warm red, marbled with gypsum bands, and from half-a-dozen places spurted jets of water, to fall in long cascades down its face. The swell frothed white on the flinty beach, and the water beyond where the shadows of an outstanding rock lay, was green and purple in a thousand tints and marked with streaks and flakes of foam. The air was full of sunlight and the tinkling of the little waterfalls and the slow soughing of the seas below. Now and then a butterfly flickered over the face of the cliff, and a multitude of sea birds perched and flew hither and thither.

The Angel lay with his crippled, shrivelled wings humped upon his back, watching the gulls and jackdaws and rooks, circling in the sunlight, soaring, eddying, sweeping down to the water or upward into the dazzling blue of the sky. Long the Angel lay there and watched them going to and fro on outspread wings. He watched, and as he watched them he remembered with infinite longing the rivers of starlight and the sweetness of the land from which he came. And a gull came gliding overhead, swiftly and easily, with its broad wings spreading white and fair against the blue. And suddenly a shadow came into the Angel's eyes, the sunlight left them, he thought of his own crippled pinions, and put his face upon his arm and wept.

A woman who was walking along the footpath across the Cliff Field saw only a twisted hunchback dressed in the Vicar of Siddermorton's cast-off clothes, sprawling foolishly at the edge of the cliff and with his forehead on his arm. She looked at him and looked again. "The silly creature has gone to sleep," she said, and though she had a heavy basket to carry, came towards him with an idea of waking him up. But as she drew near she saw his shoulders heave and heard the sound of his sobbing.

She stood still a minute, and her features twitched into a kind of grin. Then treading softly she turned and went back towards the pathway. " 'Tis so hard to think of anything to say," she said. "Poor afflicted soul!"

Presently the Angel ceased sobbing, and stared with a tear-stained face at the beach below him.

"This world," he said, "wraps me round and swallows me up. My wings grow shrivelled and useless. Soon I shall be nothing more than a crippled man, and I shall age, and bow myself to pain, and die… I am miserable. And I am alone."

Then he rested his chin on his hands upon the edge of the cliff, and began to think of Delia's face with the light in her eyes. The Angel felt a curious desire to go to her and tell her of his withered wings. To place his arms about her and weep for the land he had lost. "Delia!" he said to himself very softly. And presently a cloud drove in front of the sun.

CHAPTER TWENTY-FOUR

Mrs Hinijer Acts

Mrs Hinijer surprised the Vicar by tapping at his study door after tea. "Begging your pardon, Sir," said Mrs Hinijer. "But might I make so bold as to speak to you for a moment?"

"Certainly, Mrs Hinijer," said the Vicar, little dreaming of the blow that was coming. He held a letter in his hand, a very strange and disagreeable letter from his bishop, a letter that irritated and distressed him, criticising in the strongest language the guests he chose to entertain in his own house. Only a popular bishop living in a democratic age, a bishop who was still half a pedagogue, could have written such a letter.

Mrs Hinijer coughed behind her hand and struggled with some respiratory disorganisation. The Vicar felt apprehensive. Usually in their interviews he was the most disconcerted. Invariably so when the interview ended.

"Well?" he said.

"May I make so bold, sir, as to arst when Mr Angel is a-going?" (Cough.)

The Vicar started. "To ask when Mr Angel is going?" he repeated slowly to gain time. "*Another!*"

"I'm sorry, sir. But I've been used to waitin' on gentlefolks, sir; and you'd hardly imagine how it feels quite to wait on such as 'im."

"Such as…'*im!* Do I understand you, Mrs Hinijer, that you don't like Mr Angel?"

"You see, sir, before I came to you, sir, I was at Lord Dundoller's seventeen years, and you, sir – if you will excuse me – are a perfect gentleman yourself, sir – though in the Church. And then…"

"Dear, dear!" said the Vicar. "And don't you regard Mr Angel as a gentleman?"

"I'm sorry to 'ave to say it, sir."

"But what…? Dear me! Surely!"

"I'm sorry to 'ave to say it, sir. But when a party goes turning vegetarian suddenly and putting out all the cooking, and hasn't no proper luggage of his own, and borry's shirts and socks from his 'ost, and don't know no better than to try his knife at peas (as I seed my very self), and goes talking in odd corners to the housemaids, and folds up his napkin after meals, and eats with his fingers at minced veal, and plays the fiddle in the middle of the night keeping everybody awake, and stares and grins at his elders a-getting upstairs, and generally misconducts himself with things that I can scarcely tell you all, one can't help thinking, sir. Thought is free, sir, and one can't help coming to one's own conclusions. Besides which, there is talk all over the village about him – what with one thing and another. I know a gentleman when I sees a gentleman, and I know a gentleman when I don't see a gentleman, and me, and Susan, and George, we've talked it over, being the upper servants so to speak, and experienced, and leaving out that girl Delia, who I only hope

150

won't come to any harm through him, and depend upon it, sir, that Mr Angel ain't what you think he is, sir, and the sooner he leaves this house the better."

Mrs Hinijer ceased abruptly and stood panting but stern, and with her eyes grimly fixed on the Vicar's face.

"*Really*, Mrs Hinijer!" said the Vicar, and then, "Oh *Lord!*"

"What *have* I done?" said the Vicar, suddenly starting up and appealing to the inexorable fates. "What *have* I done?"

"There's no knowing," said Mrs Hinijer. "Though a deal of talk in the village."

"*Bother!*" said the Vicar, going and staring out of the window. Then he turned. "Look here, Mrs Hinijer! Mr Angel will be leaving this house in the course of a week. Is that enough?"

"Quite," said Mrs Hinijer. "And I feel sure, sir…"

The Vicar's eyes fell with unwonted eloquence upon the door.

CHAPTER TWENTY-FIVE

The Angel in Trouble

"The fact is," said the Vicar, "this is no world for Angels."

The blinds had not been drawn, and the twilight outer world under an overcast sky seemed unspeakably grey and cold. The Angel sat at table in dejected silence. His inevitable departure had been proclaimed. Since his presence hurt people and made the Vicar wretched he acquiesced in the justice of the decision, but what would happen to him after his plunge he could not imagine. Something very disagreeable certainly.

"There is the violin," said the Vicar. "Only after our experience –

"I must get you clothes – a general outfit – Dear me! you don't understand railway travelling! And coinage! Taking lodgings! Eating-houses! – I must come up at least and see you settled. Get work for you. But an Angel in London! Working for his living! That grey cold wilderness of people! What *will* become of you? – If I had one friend in the world I could trust to believe me!

"I ought not to be sending you away – "

"Do not trouble overmuch for me, my friend," said the Angel. "At least this life of yours ends. And there are things in it. There

153

is something in this life of yours – Your care for me! I thought there was nothing beautiful at all in life – "

"And I have betrayed you!" said the Vicar, with a sudden wave of remorse. "Why did I not face them all – say, 'This is the best of life'? What do these everyday things matter?"

He stopped suddenly. "What *do* they matter?" he said.

"I have only come into your life to trouble it," said the Angel.

"Don't say that," said the Vicar. "You have come into my life to awaken me. I have been dreaming – dreaming. Dreaming this was necessary and that. Dreaming that this narrow prison was the world. And the dream still hangs about me and troubles me. That is all. Even your departure –. Am I not dreaming that you must go?"

When he was in bed that night the mystical aspect of the case came still more forcibly before the Vicar. He lay awake and had the most horrible visions of his sweet and delicate visitor drifting through this unsympathetic world and happening upon the cruellest misadventures. His guest *was* an Angel assuredly. He tried to go over the whole story of the past eight days again. He thought of the hot afternoon, the shot fired out of sheer surprise, the fluttering iridescent wings, the beautiful saffron-robed figure upon the ground. How wonderful that had seemed to him! Then his mind turned to the things he had heard of the other world, to the dreams the violin had conjured up, to the vague, fluctuating, wonderful cities of the Angelic Land. He tried to recall the forms of the buildings, the shapes of the fruits upon the trees, the aspect of the winged shapes that traversed its ways. They grew from a memory into a present reality, grew every moment just a little more vivid and his troubles a little less immediate; and so, softly and quietly, the Vicar slipped out of his troubles and perplexities into the Land of Dreams.

2

Delia sat with her window open, hoping to hear the Angel play. But that night there was to be no playing. The sky was overcast, yet not so thickly but that the moon was visible. High up a broken cloud-lace drove across the sky, and now the moon was a hazy patch of light, and now it was darkened, and now rode clear and bright and sharply outlined against the blue gulf of night. And presently she heard the door into the garden opening, and a figure came out under the drifting pallor of the moonlight.

It was the Angel. But he wore once more the saffron robe in the place of his formless overcoat. In the uncertain light this garment had only a colourless shimmer, and his wings behind him seemed a leaden grey. He began taking short runs, flapping his wings and leaping, going to and fro amidst the drifting patches of light and the shadows of the trees. Delia watched him in amazement. He gave a despondent cry, leaping higher. His shrivelled wings flashed and fell. A thicker patch in the cloud-film made everything obscure. He seemed to spring five or six feet from the ground and fall clumsily. She saw him in the dimness crouching on the ground and then she heard him sobbing.

"He's hurt!" said Delia, pressing her lips together hard and staring. "I ought to help him."

She hesitated, then stood up and flitted swiftly towards the door, went slipping quietly downstairs and out into the moonlight. The Angel still lay upon the lawn, and sobbed for utter wretchedness.

"Oh! what is the matter?" said Delia, stooping over him and touching his head timidly.

The Angel ceased sobbing, sat up abruptly, and stared at her. He saw her face, moonlit, and soft with pity. "What is the matter?" she whispered. "Are you hurt?"

The Angel stared about him, and his eyes came to rest on her face. "Delia!" he whispered.

"Are you hurt?" said Delia.

"My wings," said the Angel. "I cannot use my wings."

Delia did not understand, but she realised that it was something very dreadful. "It is dark, it is cold," whispered the Angel; "I cannot use my wings."

It hurt her unaccountably to see the tears on his face. She did not know what to do.

"Pity me, Delia," said the Angel, suddenly extending his arms towards her; "pity me."

Impulsively she knelt down and took his face between her hands. "I do not know," she said; "but I am sorry. I am sorry for you, with all my heart."

The Angel said not a word. He was looking at her little face in the bright moonlight, with an expression of uncomprehending wonder in his eyes. "This strange world!" he said.

She suddenly withdrew her hands. A cloud drove over the moon. 'What can I do to help you?" she whispered. "I would do anything to help you."

He still held her at arm's length, perplexity replacing misery in his face. "This strange world!" he repeated.

Both whispered, she kneeling, he sitting, in the fluctuating moonlight and darkness of the lawn.

"Delia!" said Mrs Hinijer, suddenly projecting from her window; "Delia, is that you?"

They both looked up at her in consternation.

"Come in at once, Delia," said Mrs Hinijer. "If that Mr Angel was a gentleman (which he isn't), he'd feel ashamed of hisself. And you an orphan too!"

CHAPTER TWENTY-SIX

The Last Day of the Visit

On the morning of the next day the Angel, after he had breakfasted, went out towards the moor, and Mrs Hinijer had an interview with the Vicar. What happened need not concern us now. The Vicar was visibly disconcerted. "He must go," he said; "certainly he must go," and straightaway he forgot the particular accusation in the general trouble. He spent the morning in hazy meditation, interspersed by a spasmodic study of Skiff and Waterlow's price list, and the catalogue of the Medical, Scholastic, and Clerical Stores. A schedule grew slowly on a sheet of paper that lay on the desk before him. He cut out a self-measurement form from the tailoring department of the Stores and pinned it to the study curtains. This was the kind of document he was making:

"*1 Black Melton Frock Coat. patts? £3, 10s.*

"*? Trousers. 2 pairs or one.*

"*1 Cheviot Tweed Suit (write for patterns. Self-meas.?)*"

The Vicar spent some time studying a pleasing array of model gentlemen. They were all very nice-looking, but he found it hard to imagine the Angel so transfigured. For, although six days had passed, the Angel remained without any suit of his own. The

159

Vicar had vacillated between a project of driving the Angel into Portbrodock and getting him measured for a suit, and his absolute horror of the insinuating manners of the tailor he employed. He knew that tailor would demand an exhaustive explanation. Besides which, one never knew when the Angel might leave. So the six days had passed, and the Angel had grown steadily in the wisdom of this world and shrouded his brightness still in the ample retirement of the Vicar's newest clothes.

"*1 Soft Felt Hat, No. G. 7 (say), 8s 6d.*

"*1 Silk Hat, 14s 6d. Hatbox?*"

("I suppose he ought to have a silk hat," said the Vicar; "it's the correct thing up there. Shape No. 3 seems best suited to his style. But it's dreadful to think of him all alone in that great city. Everyone will misunderstand him, and he will misunderstand everybody. However, I suppose it *must* be. Where was I?")

"*1 Toothbrush. 1 Brush and Comb. Razor?*

"*$^1/_2$ doz. Shirts (? measure his neck), 6s ea.*

"*Socks? Pants?*

"*2 suits Pyjamas. Price? Say 15s.*

"*1 doz. Collars ('The Life Guardsman'), 8s.*

"*Braces. Oxon Patent Versatile, 1s 11$^1/_2$d.*" ("But how will he get them on?" said the Vicar.)

"*1 Rubber Stamp, T. Angel, and Marking Ink in box complete, 9d.*

("Those washerwomen are certain to steal all his things.")

"*1 Single-bladed Penknife with Corkscrew, say 1s 6d.*

"*N.B. – Don't forget Cuff Links, Collar Stud, &c.*" (The Vicar loved "&c.", it gave things such a precise and business-like air.)

"*1 Leather Portmanteau (had better see these).*"

And so forth – meanderingly. It kept the Vicar busy until lunch time, though his heart ached.

The Angel did not return to lunch. This was not so very remarkable – once before he had missed the midday meal. Yet, considering how short was the time they would have together now, he might perhaps have come back. Doubtless he had excellent reasons, though, for his absence. The Vicar made an indifferent lunch. In the afternoon he rested in his usual manner, and did a little more to the list of requirements. He did not begin to feel nervous about the Angel till tea-time. He waited, perhaps, half an hour before he took tea. "Odd," said the Vicar, feeling still more lonely as he drank his tea.

As the time for dinner crept on and no Angel appeared the Vicar's imagination began to trouble him. "He will come in to dinner, surely," said the Vicar, caressing his chin, and beginning to fret about the house upon inconsiderable errands, as his habit was when anything occurred to break his routine. The sun set, a gorgeous spectacle, amidst tumbled masses of purple cloud. The gold and red faded into twilight; the evening star gathered her robe of light together from out the brightness of the sky in the West. Breaking the silence of evening that crept over the outer world, a corncrake began his whirring chant. The Vicar's face grew troubled; twice he went and stared at the darkening hillside, and then fretted back to the house again. Mrs Hinijer served dinner. "Your dinner's ready," she announced for the second time, with a reproachful intonation. "Yes, yes," said the Vicar, fussing off upstairs.

He came down and went into his study and lit his reading lamp, a patent affair with an incandescent wick, dropping the match into his waste-paper basket without stopping to see if it was extinguished. Then he fretted into the dining-room and began a desultory attack on the cooling dinner...

(Dear Reader, the time is almost ripe to say farewell to this little Vicar of ours.)

2

Sir John Gotch (still smarting over the business of the barbed wire) was riding along one of the grassy ways through the preserves by the Sidder, when he saw, strolling slowly through the trees beyond the undergrowth, the one particular human being he did not want to see.

"I'm damned," said Sir John Gotch, with immense emphasis; "if this isn't altogether too much."

He raised himself in the stirrups. "Hi!" he shouted. "You there!"

The Angel turned smiling.

"Get out of this wood!" said Sir John Gotch.

"*Why?*" said the Angel.

"I'm – ," said Sir John Gotch, meditating some cataclysmal expletive. But he could think of nothing more than "damned." "Get out of this wood," he said.

The Angel's smile vanished. "Why should I get out of this wood?" he said, and stood still.

Neither spoke for a full half minute perhaps, and then Sir John Gotch dropped out of his saddle and stood by the horse.

(Now you must remember – lest the Angelic Hosts be discredited hereby – that this Angel had been breathing the poisonous air of this Struggle for Existence of ours for more than a week. It was not only his wings and the brightness of his face that suffered. He had eaten and slept and learnt the lesson of pain – had travelled so far on the road to humanity. All the length of his Visit he had been meeting more and more of the harshness and conflict of this world, and losing touch with the glorious altitudes of his own.)

"You won't go, eigh!" said Gotch, and began to lead his horse through the bushes towards the Angel. The Angel stood, all his muscles tight and his nerves quivering, watching his antagonist approach.

"Get out of this wood," said Gotch, stopping three yards away, his face white with rage, his bridle in one hand and his riding whip in the other.

Strange floods of emotion were running through the Angel. "Who are you," he said, in a low quivering voice; "who am I – that you should order me out of this place? What has the World done that men like you…"

"You're the fool who cut my barbed wire," said Gotch, threatening, "If you want to know!"

"*Your* barbed wire," said the Angel. "Was that your barbed wire? Are you the man who put down that barbed wire? What right have you…"

"Don't you go talking Socialist rot," said Gotch in short gasps. "This wood's mine, and I've a right to protect it how I can. I know your kind of muck. Talking rot and stirring up discontent. And if you don't get out of it jolly sharp…"

"*Well!*" said the Angel, a brimming reservoir of unaccountable energy.

"Get out of this damned wood!" said Gotch, flashing into the bully out of sheer alarm at the light in the Angel's face.

He made one step towards him, with the whip raised, and then something happened that neither he nor the Angel properly understood. The Angel seemed to leap into the air, a pair of grey wings flashed out at the Squire, he saw a face bearing down upon him, full of the wild beauty of passionate anger. His riding whip was torn out of his hand. His horse reared behind him, pulled him over, gained his bridle and fled.

The whip cut across his face as he fell back, stung across his face again as he sat on the ground. He saw the Angel, radiant with anger, in the act to strike again. Gotch flung up his hands, pitched himself forward to save his eyes, and rolled on the ground under the pitiless fury of the blows that rained down upon him.

"You brute," cried the Angel, striking wherever he saw flesh to feel. "You bestial thing of pride and lies! You who have overshadowed the souls of other men. You shallow fool with your horses and dogs! To lift your face against any living thing! Learn! Learn! Learn!"

Gotch began screaming for help. Twice he tried to clamber to his feet, got to his knees, and went headlong again under the ferocious anger of the Angel. Presently he made a strange noise in his throat, and ceased even to writhe under his punishment.

Then suddenly the Angel awakened from his wrath, and found himself standing, panting and trembling, one foot on a motionless figure, under the green stillness of the sunlit woods.

He stared about him, then down at his feet where, among the tangled dead leaves, the hair was matted with blood. The whip dropped from his hands, the hot colour fled from his face. "*Pain!*" he said. "Why does he lie so still?"

He took his foot off Gotch's shoulder, bent down towards the prostrate figure, stood listening, knelt – shook him. "Awake!" said the Angel. Then still more softly, "*Awake!*"

He remained listening some minutes or more, stood up sharply, and looked round him at the silent trees. A feeling of profound horror descended upon him, wrapped him round about. With an abrupt gesture he turned. "What has happened to me?" he said, in an awe-stricken whisper.

He started back from the motionless figure. "*Dead!*" he said suddenly, and turning, panic-stricken, fled headlong through the wood.

3

It was some minutes after the footsteps of the Angel had died away in the distance that Gotch raised himself on his hand. "By Jove!" he said. "Crump's right.

"Cut at the head, too!"

He put his hand to his face and felt the two weals running across it, hot and fat. "I'll think twice before I lift my hand against a lunatic again," said Sir John Gotch.

"He may be a person of weak intellect, but I'm damned if he hasn't a pretty strong arm. *Phew!* He's cut a bit clean off the top of my ear with that infernal lash.

"That infernal horse will go galloping to the house in the approved dramatic style. Little Madam'll be scared out of her wits. And I... I shall have to explain how it all happened. While she vivisects me with questions.

"I'm a jolly good mind to have spring guns and man-traps put in this preserve. Confound the Law!"

4

But the Angel, thinking that Gotch was dead, went wandering off in a passion of remorse and fear through the brakes and copses along the Sidder. You can scarcely imagine how appalled he was at this last and overwhelming proof of his encroaching humanity. All the darkness, passion and pain of life seemed closing in upon him, inexorably, becoming part of him, chaining him to all that a week ago he had found strange and pitiful in men.

"Truly, this is no world for an Angel!" said the Angel. "It is a World of War, a World of Pain, a World of Death. Anger comes upon one... I who knew not pain and anger, stand here with blood stains on my hands. I have fallen. To come into this world is to fall. One must hunger and thirst and be tormented with a thousand desires. One must fight for foothold, be angry and strike – "

He lifted up his hands to Heaven, the ultimate bitterness of helpless remorse in his face, and then flung them down with a gesture of despair. The prison walls of this narrow passionate life seemed creeping in upon him, certainly and steadily, to crush him presently altogether. He felt what all we poor mortals have to feel sooner or later – the pitiless force of the Things that Must Be, not only without us but (where the real trouble lies) within, all the inevitable tormenting of one's high resolves, those inevitable seasons when the better self is forgotten. But with us it is a gentle descent, made by imperceptible degrees over a long space of years; with him it was the horrible discovery of one short week. He felt he was being crippled, caked over, blinded, stupefied in the wrappings of this life, he felt as a man might feel who has taken some horrible poison, and feels destruction spreading within him.

He took no account of hunger or fatigue or the flight of time. On and on he went, avoiding houses and roads, turning away from the sight and sound of a human being in a wordless desperate argument with Fate. His thoughts did not flow but stood banked back in inarticulate remonstrance against his degradation. Chance directed his footsteps homeward and, at last, after nightfall, he found himself faint and weary and wretched, stumbling along over the moor at the back of Siddermorton. He heard the rats run and squeal in the heather, and once a noiseless big bird came out of the darkness, passed, and vanished again. And he saw without noticing it a dull red glow in the sky before him.

5

But when he came over the brow of the moor, a vivid light sprang up before him and refused to be ignored. He came on down the hill and speedily saw more distinctly what the glare was. It came from darting and trembling tongues of fire, golden and red, that shot from the windows and a hole in the roof of the Vicarage. A cluster of black heads, all the village in fact, except the fire-brigade – who were down at Aylmer's Cottage trying to find the key of the machine-house – came out in silhouette against the blaze. There was a roaring sound, and a humming of voices, and presently a furious outcry. There was a shouting of "No! No!" – "Come back!" and an inarticulate roar.

He began to run towards the burning house. He stumbled and almost fell, but he ran on. He found black figures running about him. The flaring fire blew gustily this way and that, and he smelt the smell of burning.

"She went in," said one voice, "she went in."

"The mad girl!" said another.

"Stand back! Stand back!" cried others.

He found himself thrusting through an excited, swaying crowd, all staring at the flames, and with the red reflection in their eyes.

"Stand back!" said a labourer, clutching him.

"What is it?" said the Angel. "What does this mean?"

"There's a girl in the house, and she can't get out!"

"Went in after a fiddle," said another.

" 'Tas hopeless," he heard someone else say.

"I was standing near her. I heerd her. Says she: 'I *can* get his fiddle.' I heerd her – Just like that! 'I *can* get his fiddle.' "

For a moment the Angel stood staring. Then in a flash he saw it all, saw this grim little world of battle and cruelty, transfigured in a splendour that outshone the Angelic Land, suffused suddenly and insupportably glorious with the wonderful light of Love and Self-Sacrifice. He gave a strange cry, and before anyone could stop him, was running towards the burning building. There were cries of "The Hunchback! The Fowener!"

The Vicar, whose scalded hand was being tied up, turned his head, and he and Crump saw the Angel, a black outline against the intense, red glare of the doorway. It was the sensation of the tenth of a second, yet both men could not have remembered that transitory attitude more vividly had it been a picture they had studied for hours together. Then the Angel was hidden by something massive (no one knew what) that fell, incandescent, across the doorway.

6

There was a cry of "Delia" and no more. But suddenly the flames spurted out in a blinding glare that shot upward to an immense height, a blinding brilliance broken by a thousand flickering gleams like the waving of swords. And a gust of sparks, flashing in a thousand colours, whirled up and vanished. Just then, and for a moment by some strange accident, a rush of music, like the swell of an organ, wove into the roaring of the flames.

The whole village standing in black knots heard the sound, except Gaffer Siddons who is deaf – strange and beautiful it was, and then gone again. Lumpy Durgan, the idiot boy from Sidderford, said it began and ended like the opening and shutting of a door.

But little Hetty Penzance had a pretty fancy of two figures with wings, that flashed up and vanished among the flames.

(And after that it was she began to pine for the things she saw in her dreams, and was abstracted and strange. It grieved her mother sorely at the time. She grew fragile, as though she was fading out of the world, and her eyes had a strange, far-away look. She talked of angels and rainbow colours and golden wings, and was for ever singing an unmeaning fragment of an air that nobody knew. Until Crump took her in hand and cured her with fattening dietary, syrup of hypophosphites and cod liver oil.)

THE EPILOGUE

And there the story of the Wonderful Visit ends. The Epilogue is in the mouth of Mrs Mendham. There stand two little white crosses in the Siddermorton churchyard, near together, where the brambles come clambering over the stone wall. One is inscribed Thomas Angel and the other Delia Hardy, and the dates of the deaths are the same. Really there is nothing beneath them but the ashes of the Vicar's stuffed ostrich. (You will remember the Vicar had his ornithological side.) I noticed them when Mrs Mendham was showing me the new De la Beche monument. (Mendham has been Vicar since Hilyer died.) "The granite came from somewhere in Scotland," said Mrs Mendham, "and cost ever so much – I forget how much – but a wonderful lot! It's quite the talk of the village."

"Mother," said Cissie Mendham, "you are stepping on a grave."

"Dear me!" said Mrs Mendham, "How heedless of me! And the cripple's grave too. But really you've no idea how much this monument cost them."

"These two people, by the bye," said Mrs Mendham, "were killed when the old Vicarage was burnt. It's rather a strange story. He was a curious person, a hunchbacked fiddler, who came from nobody knows where, and imposed upon the late Vicar to a frightful extent. He played in a pretentious way by ear, and we found out afterwards that he did not know a note of music – not a note. He was exposed before quite a lot of people. Among other things, he seems to have been 'carrying on,' as people say, with one of the servants, a sly little drab… But Mendham had better tell you all about it. The man was half-witted and curiously deformed. It's strange the fancies girls have."

She looked sharply at Cissie, and Cissie blushed to the eyes.

"She was left in the house and he rushed into the flames in an attempt to save her. Quite romantic – isn't it? He was rather clever with the fiddle in his uneducated way.

"All the poor Vicar's stuffed skins were burned at the same time. It was almost all he cared for. He never really got over the blow. He came to stop with us – for there wasn't another house available in the village. But he never seemed happy. He seemed all shaken. I never saw a man so changed. I tried to stir him up, but it was no good – no good at all. He had the queerest delusions about angels and that kind of thing. It made him odd company at times. He would say he heard music, and stare quite stupidly at nothing for hours together. He got quite careless about his dress… He died within a twelvemonth of the fire."

H G WELLS

THE HISTORY OF MR POLLY

Mr Polly is one of literature's most enduring and universal creations. An ordinary man, trapped in an ordinary life, Mr Polly makes a series of ill-advised choices that bring him to the very brink of financial ruin. Determined not to become the latest victim of the economic retrenchment of the Edwardian age, he rebels in magnificent style and takes control of his life once and for all.

ISBN 0-7551-0404-8

H G WELLS

IN THE DAYS OF THE COMET

Revenge was all Leadford could think of as he set out to find the unfaithful Nettie and her adulterous lover. But this was all to change when a new comet entered the earth's orbit and totally reversed the natural order of things. The Great Change had occurred and any previous emotions, thoughts, ambitions, hopes and fears had all been removed. Free love, pacifism and equality were now the name of the game. But how would Leadford fare in this most utopian of societies?

ISBN 0-7551-0406-4

H G WELLS

THE INVISIBLE MAN

On a cold wintry day in the depths of February a stranger appeared in The Coach and Horses requesting a room. So strange was this man's appearance, dressed from head to foot with layer upon layer of clothing, bandages and the most enormous glasses, that the owner, Mrs Hall, quite wondered what accident could have befallen him. She didn't know then that he was invisible – but the rumours soon began to spread…

H G Wells' masterpiece *The Invisible Man* is a classic science-fiction thriller showing the perils of scientific advancement.

ISBN 0-7551-0407-2

H G WELLS

THE ISLAND OF DR MOREAU

A shipwreck in the South Seas brings a doctor to an island paradise. Far from seeing this as the end of his life, Dr Moreau seizes the opportunity to play God and infiltrate a reign of terror in this new kingdom. Endless cruel and perverse experiments ensue and see a series of new creations – the 'Beast People' – all of which must bow before the deified doctor.

Originally a Swiftian satire on the dangers of authority and submission, Wells' *The Island of Dr Moreau* can now just as well be read as a prophetic tale of genetic modification and mutability.

ISBN 0-7551-0408-0

H G WELLS

MEN LIKE GODS

Mr Barnstaple was ever such a careful driver, careful to indicate before every manoeuvre and very much in favour of slowing down at the slightest hint of difficulty. So however could he have got the car into a skid on a bend on the Maidenhead road?

When he recovered himself he was more than a little relieved to see the two cars that he had been following still merrily motoring along in front of him. It seemed that all was well – except that the scenery had changed, rather a lot. It was then that the awful truth dawned: Mr Barnstaple had been hurled into another world altogether.

How would he ever survive in this supposed Utopia, and more importantly, how would he ever get back?

ISBN 0-7551-0413-7

H G WELLS

THE WAR OF THE WORLDS

'No one would have believed in the last years of the nineteenth century that this world was being watched keenly and closely by intelligences greater than man's…'

A series of strange atmospheric disturbances on the planet Mars may raise concern on Earth but it does little to prepare the inhabitants for imminent invasion. At first the odd-looking Martians seem to pose no threat for the intellectual powers of Victorian London, but it seems man's superior confidence is disastrously misplaced. For the Martians are heading towards victory with terrifying velocity.

The War of the Worlds is an expertly crafted invasion story that can be read as a frenzied satire on the dangers of imperialism and occupation.

ISBN 0-7551-0426-9

OTHER TITLES BY H G WELLS AVAILABLE DIRECT
FROM HOUSE OF STRATUS

Quantity	£	$(US)	$(CAN)	€
FICTION				
ANN VERONICA	9.99	14.95	22.95	16.50
APROPOS OF DOLORES	9.99	14.95	22.95	16.50
THE AUTOCRACY OF MR PARHAM	9.99	14.95	22.95	16.50
BABES IN THE DARKLING WOOD	9.99	14.95	22.95	16.50
BEALBY	9.99	14.95	22.95	16.50
THE BROTHERS AND				
THE CROQUET PLAYER	7.99	12.95	19.95	14.50
BRYNHILD	9.99	14.95	22.95	16.50
THE BULPINGTON OF BLUP	9.99	14.95	22.95	16.50
THE DREAM	9.99	14.95	22.95	16.50
THE FIRST MEN IN THE MOON	9.99	14.95	22.95	16.50
THE FOOD OF THE GODS	9.99	14.95	22.95	16.50
THE HISTORY OF MR POLLY	9.99	14.95	22.95	16.50
THE HOLY TERROR	9.99	14.95	22.95	16.50
IN THE DAYS OF THE COMET	9.99	14.95	22.95	16.50
THE INVISIBLE MAN	7.99	12.95	19.95	14.50
THE ISLAND OF DR MOREAU	7.99	12.95	19.95	14.50
KIPPS: THE STORY OF A SIMPLE SOUL	9.99	14.95	22.95	16.50
LOVE AND MR LEWISHAM	9.99	14.95	22.95	16.50
MARRIAGE	9.99	14.95	22.95	16.50
MEANWHILE	9.99	14.95	22.95	16.50
MEN LIKE GODS	9.99	14.95	22.95	16.50
A MODERN UTOPIA	9.99	14.95	22.95	16.50
MR BRITLING SEES IT THROUGH	9.99	14.95	22.95	16.50

ALL HOUSE OF STRATUS BOOKS ARE AVAILABLE FROM GOOD BOOKSHOPS
OR DIRECT FROM THE PUBLISHER:

Internet: www.houseofstratus.com including synopses and features.

Email: sales@houseofstratus.com
info@houseofstratus.com
(please quote author, title and credit card details.)

OTHER TITLES BY H G WELLS AVAILABLE DIRECT
FROM HOUSE OF STRATUS

Quantity	£	$(US)	$(CAN)	€
FICTION				
THE NEW MACHIAVELLI	9.99	14.95	22.95	16.50
THE PASSIONATE FRIENDS	9.99	14.95	22.95	16.50
THE SEA LADY	7.99	12.95	19.95	14.50
THE SHAPE OF THINGS TO COME	9.99	14.95	22.95	16.50
THE TIME MACHINE	7.99	12.95	19.95	14.50
TONO-BUNGAY	9.99	14.95	22.95	16.50
THE UNDYING FIRE	7.99	12.95	19.95	14.50
THE WAR IN THE AIR	9.99	14.95	22.95	16.50
THE WAR OF THE WORLDS	7.99	12.95	19.95	14.50
THE WHEELS OF CHANCE	7.99	12.95	19.95	14.50
WHEN THE SLEEPER WAKES	9.99	14.95	22.95	16.50
THE WIFE OF SIR ISAAC HARMAN	9.99	14.95	22.95	16.50
THE WORLD OF WILLIAM CLISSOLD				
VOLUMES 1,2,3	12.99	19.95	29.95	22.00
NON-FICTION				
THE CONQUEST OF TIME *AND*				
THE HAPPY TURNING	7.99	12.95	19.95	14.50
EXPERIMENT IN AUTOBIOGRAPHY				
VOLUMES 1,2	12.99	19.95	29.95	22.00
H G WELLS IN LOVE	9.99	14.95	22.95	16.50
THE OPEN CONSPIRACY AND				
OTHER WRITINGS	9.99	14.95	22.95	16.50

Tel:	Order Line		International	
	0800 169 1780 (UK)		+44 (0) 1845 527700 (UK)	
	800 724 1100 (USA)		+01	845 463 1100 (USA)

Fax: +44 (0) 1845 527711 (UK)
      +01   845 463 0018 (USA)
      (please quote author, title and credit card details.)

Send to: House of Stratus Sales Department   House of Stratus Inc.
          Thirsk Industrial Park   2 Neptune Road
          York Road, Thirsk   Poughkeepsie
          North Yorkshire, YO7 3BX   NY 12601
          UK   USA

PAYMENT (Please tick currency you wish to use):

☐ £ (Sterling) ☐ $ (US) ☐ $ (CAN) ☐ € (Euros)

Allow for shipping costs charged per order plus an amount per book as set out in the tables below:

CURRENCY/DESTINATION

	£(Sterling)	$(US)	$(CAN)	€(Euros)
Cost per order				
UK	1.50	2.25	3.50	2.50
Europe	3.00	4.50	6.75	5.00
North America	3.00	3.50	5.25	5.00
Rest of World	3.00	4.50	6.75	5.00
Additional cost per book				
UK	0.50	0.75	1.15	0.85
Europe	1.00	1.50	2.25	1.70
North America	1.00	1.00	1.50	1.70
Rest of World	1.50	2.25	3.50	3.00

PLEASE SEND CHEQUE OR INTERNATIONAL MONEY ORDER
payable to: HOUSE OF STRATUS LTD or HOUSE OF STRATUS INC. or card payment as indicated

STERLING EXAMPLE

Cost of book(s):..................... Example: 3 x books at £6.99 each: £20.97

Cost of order: .... Example: £1.50 (Delivery to UK address)

Additional cost per book:.............. Example: 3 x £0.50: £1.50

Order total including shipping:.......... Example: £23.97

VISA, MASTERCARD, SWITCH, AMEX:

☐☐☐☐☐☐☐☐☐☐☐☐☐☐☐☐☐☐☐☐☐☐

**Issue number
(Switch only):**   **Start Date:**   **Expiry Date:**

☐☐☐   ☐☐/☐☐   ☐☐/☐☐

Signature: _____

NAME: _____

ADDRESS: _____

COUNTRY: _____

ZIP/POSTCODE: _____

Please allow 28 days for delivery. Despatch normally within 48 hours.
Prices subject to change without notice.
Please tick box if you do not wish to receive any additional information. ☐

House of Stratus publishes many other titles in this genre; please check our
website (**www.houseofstratus.com**) for more details.